Notting Hill Editions is an independent British publisher. The company was founded by Tom Kremer (1930–2017), champion of innovation and the man responsible for popularising the Rubik's Cube.

After a successful business career in toy invention Tom decided, at the age of eighty, to fulfil his passion for literature. In a fast-moving digital world Tom's aim was to revive the art of the essay, and to create exceptionally beautiful books that would be lingered over and cherished.

Hailed as 'the shape of things to come', the family-run press brings to print the most surprising thinkers of past and present. In an era of information-overload, these collectible pocket-size books distil ideas that linger in the mind.

nottinghilleditions.com

Todd McEwen was born in Southern California in the 1950s. As a child he was interested in comedy and the undersea realm, and terrified by *Bambi*. In high school he had his own radio show, interviewing folk singers and puzzle inventors. At university he read Victorian and medieval English literature. He worked in radio, theatre and the rare books trade before arriving in Scotland in the 1980s. After a spell at *Granta*, he has often worked as an editor and teacher. His novels include *Fisher's Hornpipe*, *McX: A Romance of the Dour*, *Who Sleeps with Katz* and *The Five Simple Machines*.

CARY GRANT'S SUIT

Nine Movies that Made Me
the Wreck I Am Today

–

Todd McEwen

ηh Notting Hill Editions

Published in 2023
by Notting Hill Editions Ltd
Mirefoot, Burneside, Kendal LA8 9AB

Series design by FLOK Design, Berlin, Germany
Cover design by Tom Etherington
Creative Advisor: Dennis PAPHITIS

Typeset by CB Editions, London
Printed and bound by
Memminger MedienCentrum, Memmingen, Germany

A CIP record for this book is available from the British Library

ISBN 978-1-912559-40-4

nottinghilleditions.com

For Patchy,
with love

The great miraculous event, half sunset half sunrise, with the intervening night displaced, would start to unfold. The lights dimmed, a hush, like the end of the day, fell on the audience, and the first titles came up on the screen, and they could, just for a moment, be seen, the far side of the gauze curtains, as clear as pebbles through still water.

– Richard Wollheim, *Germs*

People always think something's *all* true.

– J. D. Salinger

Contents

— I Am Sucked into the System —

In the middle of *Bambi* I started to scream and wouldn't stop. I had to be removed and then hosed down. Is this any way to begin one's movie-going life?

Getting used to the movies was like learning to drink coffee or to smoke. You never knew when something adult and horrible was going to rush at you off the screen and make you feel parentless, powerless in the middle of a black ocean, where home was far away and there was only the occasional cynical usher and his conical orange flashlight.

In *Tomahawk* I was confronted with a twenty-foot high Navajo's breast-plate, seemingly made out of bleached chicken bones, from which a huge arrow was protruding and blood gushed. In *Lemonade Joe*, after the typical Western saloon fight, the town's undertaker came in, selected a corkscrew from the bar, twisted it straight into a dead cowboy, and carried him outside as if he were a Gladstone bag.

I was born the year *Shane* was released. Still, they wouldn't even allow me a *cap* gun. Not at birth of course but four or five years later, when I really needed one. When I realized what our neighborhood was: a desert, a jungle, a swamp, a menacing fairyland, outer

1

space, a prison, a marital bed, a theater of war. All danger. **They** were never going to understand; *they* were never going to help. They gave me a baby sister. I've had to use her ever since as a human shield.

On our street, there were only three games: Cowboys, Baseball and War. Just like in America. But this trio of crap began to be eroded. We gradually spent more time in front of the television, which had ever more weird and ever more stupid stuff on it. We began spilling our subconscious seed all over the street, making strange, evanescent, theatrical things – much as we'd make a 'skeleton' on the sidewalk, running through lawn sprinklers half naked and then lying down for a few seconds on the hot concrete. This gave a dark, Rorschachy suggestion of yourself, which you'd stand on and watch quickly disappear.

What we had to do was recreate instantly what we saw on television or at the movies. Had to!, with searing attention to detail, not just fall into some vague game of Boot Hill or Burma Road. Baseball all but disappeared, except for a pack of buck-toothed goofballs who lived on Clark Street.

We were children, this much was apparent; we knew we were having a childhood, but we kept seeking models for it. Our parents, their own lives interrupted, capped, sealed by war, had forgotten to tell us what . . .

I was confused by what we were shown with particular assiduousness by afternoon television 'hosts', a frightening bunch of adults who'd be thrown in jail today for the ingenuity of the methods they used to appeal to us, posing as children, sailors, firemen, jovial 'uncles' with prizes, secret words, *candy* . . . You'd be lucky to escape with your life from their fake submarines, fake garages, fake circus tents. We were being 'groomed'. For what? To be the suckers we've become, of course.

What looked a little too real, we found, a little too polished, in something purporting to *be* real, was transformed by our own efforts to realize it into something *surreal*. Which provided us with only disappointment and frustration and unhappiness. Spanky, Alfalfa and Darla were having an endless childhood in a parallel universe we couldn't get at, for all our powers of imitation, which grew and grew until as young adults we achieved the power to ignore the real world entirely. The triumph of our generation.

Although from a booky family, I was reviled for it and got sucked into the system of images first. Our exposure to books at school was execrable. The movies we'd seen by the age of ten were much better than the books we'd read. I can remember reading very few books in my school except an appalling thing about a boy who is blinded by a firework and goes all petulant (*Follow My Leader*), *Julius Caesar* (not for kids, let's face it), two war novels (*God is My Co-Pilot* and *The Bridges at Toko-Ri*), and something called *Hot Rod*. Can you imagine studying *Hot Rod* for half a year? If books really are dying, these should be among the first.

I took in rather too much about the *act* of going to the movies for my father's liking. I dawdled under the hundreds of tiny light bulbs in the marquee, I gawped at the ticket machine. I took my time breathing in the mammalian smells of the thick, old-fashioned carpeting on the stairs . . . why not? This had become my church.

But my worship was not always cinematic. I once watched *The Flintstones*, in Sacramento, four times in a row, purely for the sake of the air conditioning. Similarly overheated in Paris, I watched a lot of Gene Tierney. A little cinema in the rue Christine had the strange habit of running American movies which, really, *nobody* could possibly care about any more. The air conditioning was equally abstruse, and I had to watch most of *Leave Her to Heaven* before I felt cool. Not in the St-Germain sense. Gene Tierney rode a horse and there were it seemed acres of her face. This was also one of those pictures where you have to watch Vincent Price struggling to act *normal*; I mean before he gave it up. It's really unsettling to have to believe in him as a lawyer, pushing his big shoulders around the room in a post-war sport jacket that looks like a goddamn sofa. You keep thinking he'll bust all the finely turned chair legs in the ranch house.

I was once in a huge cinema on 57th Street watching

a double bill, as it turned out, of *The Last Detail* and *Emmanuelle.* Who thought up *this* combo? Maybe there were sailors in town. Outside it was a chilly day in early spring and everyone in the warm theater was drowsing and snuggling in their overcoats. I don't think most of them wanted to watch *Emmanuelle* – how could they? It was just too nice and warm and difficult to leave. Halfway through the thing a guy in about row 10 fell totally and helplessly asleep, head back and mouth open, snoring loudly during a scene in which a pointy-eared slaphead ravishes Sylvia Kristel. His neighbors jostled him a little to no effect, and then people started throwing things at him, popcorn and candy and pennies, particularly from the balcony. Thinking of a way to wake this guy up had riveted the audience, they couldn't care less about soft focus buttocks . . . Then someone in back of me launched a tangerine, which not only struck his face but dropped perfectly into his open mouth and stayed there – a hole in one. Strangling, he jumped to his feet and flailed his arms, to wild applause.

– What the Outdoors Had to Offer –

T he smells of Balfour Avenue were these: fertilizer (every lawn was new), concrete (you could smell it when the sprinklers were on), grass, and an acrid odor which was the product of cars, farms, and the few small factories of our town. We made potato chips, Hawaiian Punch, tubas and electric guitars. I say we. But in those days we were all together. Supposedly.

Ours was a three-bedroom house. My parents bought it in 1955 for $14,580. There was a kitchen, a living/dining room, a 'den' and two bathrooms. There was a garage, separated from the house by a 'breeze-way'. Breezes were not included.

In the back yard were an unsuccessful banana tree, a birch, and a lot of dirt and geraniums. In the side yard were our swings. In front of the house was a curious driveway which my father had resurfaced himself; lots of sea shells were visible in the concrete. There was a plum tree that didn't bear fruit, which we decorated for the confused birds of the desert at Christmas with popcorn, dried cranberries and bacon fat.

There was the sidewalk, the location of many, or all, encounters, fantasies and dramas. There was a young liquidambar tree in a strip of grass between the

6

sidewalk and the street, uniform with every home, and there was the street.

I thought about our neighborhood in a diagrammatic way. It was so many feet to one house or another. The street curved gently, but I thought of it as straight. It took ten minutes to walk to school, where there was no vegetation.

As a child I had very little experience of shade. My parents had a practice of keeping the house dark when the weather was hot. To cool us, they put us in water: they took us to the swimming club, or plunked us in the inflatable wading pool. All the food we ate was refrigerated, all year long. I still prefer most of what I eat to be chilled.

The houses were all of a certain type: stucco and decorated wood. They looked different from each other, but really they weren't.

The street contained things. For us it was a staging area: baseball, battles, re-enactments. It was a backdrop, a 'set' – this is what your environment is when you are young, because you can't be sure of its reality, or permanence. The street was a cultural blank, on which we could write anything. The neighborhood was as blank as a Colorforms board. The street was a train track, a river, a conduit of slow-moving adults in cars (sometimes a useful obstacle if somebody was chasing you).

Several of us were admirers of the street-sweeping machine and the man who drove it. He wore gloves and a dirty hat and had a cigar in his mouth. But what was there for the machine to suck up? There was never anything in the gutters, no trash, no leaves. After the machine passed by, the street was slightly wet, and we really liked that smell. It was different from the wet sidewalk smell.

I was submerged, I was muffled. I felt I couldn't get *at* anything. I found it hard to connect with anyone. Debbie was OK. And later, Fard. With everyone else on the street I had either an uncomprehending relationship or a potentially fractious one steeped in fear.

The neighborhood was not an especially poor or violent one. I didn't get beaten up nearly as often as I thought I was going to. In my own way I developed a love of wildness, of trespass. Not of violence. I was not in favor of violence. Even I could see that Charlie Chaplin sticking a fork in someone's butt would be painful; that if Tom really did that to Jerry they'd be scraping him off the road. There was a lot of post-war violence hanging around us kids. There was a contingent in the neighborhood that would only play war. These endless pantomime machine-gunnings of each other didn't interest me as I didn't know the conventions, not watching war movies. Nor was I allowed to own a toy gun. So here was another *blow to camaraderie.*

Model building was big – battleships and fighter planes. The brothers next door had a virtual air force hanging by nylon threads from the ceiling. You felt like you were under aerial attack if you walked into their bedroom.

Let's say it was early on a Saturday morning. It almost never rained, it was almost never cloudy, but say it was overcast. Our neighborhood was quiet enough, although we were becoming used to noise: ever more traffic. The droning of airplanes. But an overcast day was so unusual, it held a special excitement. You heard, noticed things more.

It felt natural, best, to be awake in the house on such a morning. Coolness felt right; the air seemed to move in the early mornings and then to stop for the rest of the day. Sometimes the only thing you heard was the hissing and dripping of sprinklers. There was a kind that went back and forth like a fan, there was a kind that looked like the eyes of an owl, and there was a kind that you just stuck in the ground with a long rusty spike and had to go out and move every twenty minutes.

I would have been sleeping with just a sheet over me. I had nylon pajamas with short sleeves and snaps. I was the worst sleeper in the family. I always got up early on weekends because the day promised something, even if the others weren't going to be up for hours. I liked the smells and the coolness. I went to the kitchen for cereal and milk. Then I went to the den. What else would you expect?

Our TV was a DuMont, now an extinct name, though it was even a television network at one time.

But it stands to reason they'd never get away with that, naming a TV network after yourself. People were going to be electrified only by three-letter zappy names. CBS! ABC! NBC! 'Mutual' was doomed, obviously. (Later Ted Turner tried to get everyone to call his company 'TBS', but it didn't work. And neither do fictitious names of broadcasting companies – UBS in *Network*, for example, FBC in *Desk Set*, IBC in *Scrooged* – it's not believable. It *jolts*. Everyone just lay down in front of this charmed, malevolent trinity. And now there is MSNBC – forget it.)

This TV was a cube of maroon masonite, about two feet square. The screen was a stubby rectangle with rounded edges, mounted behind glass and edged with a dull, gold-colored aluminum strip. On the front, below the screen, were two big knobs, and two big knobs only: the knob that turned it on and regulated the volume, and the channel knob. The channel knob was illuminated for part of its life, but like many electrical niceties of the 1950s, this little bit of magic soon departed. Is this something you would ring a repairman for? The little numbers don't light up anymore? Nah. On the side of the set were vents so it could breathe, and a speaker covered with the usual 50s grille cloth, brown stuff with metallic thread in it.

The back of the DuMont was frightening and I never wanted to look at it. There was a Bakelite cup that retained the end of the cathode-ray tube, and glimpses to be had of the array of vacuum tubes and very large capacitors – when the set was turned on it looked like a city in hell.

I'm describing our TV in this way because I wish to *absolve* it – this particular TV – from participating in what TV became. I liked this modest maroon TV because of what it gave me, at that time: the history of the movies. And then, later, TV was the destroyer of that and of every other form of art. Of course, compared to the web, TV looks pretty feeble in that respect.

Televisions used to have to warm up after you turned them on. It was a short but intense period of a certain anxiety. Do you remember wondering if you were going to get the channel you wanted? Sometimes it just didn't happen. For reasons of the gods or the ether.

Channel 2 was what I needed. *Need* – think about it. Channel 2. Did I have an inbuilt clock? How was I able to do this so precisely every Saturday morning? Compulsion? Escape!

I don't have to tell you that most of the people now running the country got up early on Saturday mornings and watched television. It went on for hours, it went on for years. But I got up especially early, for Commander Rip Tide. Ostensibly in a submarine, the genial Commander would blather a bit and then pull down his periscope. He'd scan the surface of the sea (a film clip).

And then, ahoy! Ahoy what? Ahoy *not* the cartoons the primitiveness of which made my father blanch if he put his nose into the den – *I can't believe you're watching that* – and ahoy *not* the stuff that came mid-morning that we took in our stride (*The Magic Land of Alakazam*, *The Jetsons*, *Sky King*), but ahoy two hours of LAUREL AND HARDY. Ahoy. I loved it so much I thought it was broadcast just to me.

I was a submerged boy. Submerged culturally in the middle of Orange County, never close enough to the ocean, which teemed with life. I'd read all about it. But I was no slouch. For the first ten years of my life, aside from television, I spent all my time outdoors. In the summers I did not know a shirt. I was brown as a nut. You ought to see me now. I read books and I had odd thoughts that nobody understood. If I'd had a periscope like Commander Rip Tide's in my bedroom, what would I not have sighted! Yes, to *pull down my periscope*. I'd have seen enemy craft, the Ditti family across the street, preparing to attack me in some way. Billy Turley swinging a cat by its tail. Several billows away, John Jordan's house with its black cat and its orange cat. In the other direction, *Debbie's* house. Then Fard's. (Come to think of it, I befriended only people to the east of our house.) I would have been able to explore the back alley, where we were never allowed to set foot – a rakish land of incinerators and fast-moving garbage collectors. With cigars. I could have known, seen everything.

But I was submerged. And I really needed to laugh. A lot.

– *Blotto* –

To live in Southern California in the 1950s was to live in the heart of the transitory. Our parents were keen on the 'normal', trying to leave the war behind. We, on the other hand, were being prepared for the abnormal, even for chaos.

I've always been captivated by titles, openings, emblazonments, front covers, title pages and doors, especially double doors. When I watched the opening of a Laurel & Hardy movie, I was ecstatic. This cuckoo music and this faux marble plaque, or more important this painting of two derbies on a hat rack, this mesmerizing stuff, *that already I could not live without*, seemed to me as though it must have been going on forever. In some unimportant ways it seemed old, but for the most part I identified with it utterly. To think now that *Blotto* was made only twenty-odd years before I was born – and that in just a few more it will be a hundred years old.

Derbies fried my brain. If we drove through Hollywood I craned for a view of the Brown Derby restaurant, which was shaped like an enormous derby and had a small derby-shaped sign on top: EAT IN THE HAT. The first time I saw a guy actually wearing

13

a derby, at an amusement park, my jaw hit the floor. I was given a *plastic* derby for Christmas and wore it until it disintegrated. That was a bleak day. Once my grandfather took me into his bedroom and got out two carefully preserved hat boxes. In one was a straw boater with a black band, and in the other an immaculate, real derby that he had bought and worn in San Francisco in the 1920s. I couldn't believe it – my life, and Stan Laurel's life, passed before my eyes. My grandfather had kept this from me for many years.

For your information, Charlie Chaplin's derby was in no way as meaningful as Laurel's and Hardy's. People remember his waddle, his cane and his *simper* more than his derby. And that he'd stick a fork in your ass as soon as look at you.

I wasn't allowed comic books. Instead, I used to check type-design books out of the library. I was given a typewriter early in life and I liked the way it made things look. One morning my father came into my room while I was drawing at my easel, which he had made for me. He made lots of things for me, though he was puzzled as to why I wanted them. I was trying to draw the opening Laurel & Hardy title card, the one that looked like marble, although for a long time I thought it depicted a stormy sky. Appropriate. I was triply frustrated, because I didn't know how to begin drawing marble, I didn't know how to spell 'Laurel', and I had only brown crayons. Why did I only ever have brown? It was those giant boxes of Crayolas they used to give you, the ones that make you gasp on your birthday. It's just a ruse by Binney & Smith to sell off a disproportionate number of brown crayons, which are obviously the cheapest to produce and the least popular. Burnt Sienna? Mahogany? Raw Umber? Sepia? *Brown*? Nobody wants this. Everything looked like shit.

I had spelled Stan Laurel's name 'Loil'. 'HAL ROACH PRESENTS STAN LOIL AND OLIVER HARDY.' I looked at my father in consternation. 'That's a fairly difficult name to figure out how to spell,' he said. 'It's L – A – U – R – E – L .' I was really grateful, but there was nothing he could do about the brown.

One day in the 1920s my other grandfather was driving in Hollywood when he came upon the scene of an accident. A *popcorn truck* had swerved to avoid a car and overturned, spilling freshly popped corn all over the street. My grandfather pulled up and after ensuring that no one had been hurt he started gathering up the popcorn. At this point a very angry man with a megaphone ran towards him, yelling at him to get the hell out of there, couldn't he see they were making a movie? My mother kept this from me for many years. BUT WE COULDA BEEN IN THE MOVIE BUSINESS!

Laurel & Hardy: The Novel

For a long time I have thought of all of Laurel & Hardy, their *oeuvre* (and theirs was the first *oeuvre* I ever encountered) as a novel. It's a novel about Los Angeles in the 1920s and 1930s, about married life. It's certainly not about being rich – there's lots of Depression in it, unemployment and making do. It's an anti-Gatsby novel. Stan and Ollie are married to or entangled with a series of women, but they all represent the same thing: fear. Not of women exactly, well, they are pretty scared of them, but more of the physical attributes of the domestic state. The STUFF. And there is a rather beautiful explication of humanity's grappling with the electro-mechanical – in the 1920s nearly everyone had to learn how to use a radio, an automobile, a telephone. And that was often pretty funny.

The costume pictures, *Fra Diavolo*, *Babes in Toyland* and so on, aren't part of this novel, but could be the entertainments or fantasies enjoyed by the characters in the novel.

One of the most disappointing things, as it is with any series of films, is the later entries. What series of films got steadily better and better? The *Thin Man*? The *Road* movies? James Bond? Bah. The 20th Century-Fox Laurel & Hardy pictures from the 1940s are painful. Not because Laurel and Hardy are growing old, and unfunny, but because they're no longer allowed to live in *their world* – in the simple, stark Los

Angeles that favored them. In terms of *motion picture glamour* they can no longer live in little bungalows and have petty disputes and try their hands at small businesses. It would have seemed positively antique. The wives are no longer basically 'with' them, either – they're *openly hostile harried World War II women*.

This novel was about optimism. It was essentially about peacetime – think about it.

Stucco

Laurel and Hardy lived in a neighborhood like ours, or its mid-1920s equivalent. When they go up on their various roofs, to put up radio aerials or hide from their wives, I could see this. And by the way, how else would *you* dress to go businesslike about the comedy of your existence, other than in a derby, white shirt, necktie and denim overalls? Their houses were in Culver City – the vista from the roofs of those little stucco houses was of the blank canvas of a young California. And, though sun-washed, more than slightly bleak. Bleakness is a Southern California tradition. And from there it spread out to cover the whole of the United States.

I was interested in what was hidden. The roof of a house is not hidden, but it's a forbidden area, at least when you are a child. You know it covers the family – up there you could stand outwith, above your family and its day-to-day business. A roof also sports odd little pipes and vents that let things out of the family. The area underneath the house, not a cellar but a kind of crawl space, was also off-limits.

As a submerged individual I knew that being on the roof would offer perspective. I think the first time I did go up on the roof with my father I was a little too scared to go to the lip and take in the view. In the Coen brothers' movie *A Serious Man*, Michael Stuhlbarg has to go up on the roof to adjust the TV aerial so that his teenage son can watch *F-Troop* (a very Laurel & Hardy situation) and he gains the perspective, in a way – the view of the bleak sameness of the suburbs that nevertheless all the submerged hunger for. And he gets to see a naked lady!

In California the divide between what was 'inside' and what was 'outside' was blurred from the start, because of the heat: people had patios, some with shade, and large sliding doors that could open their living rooms to the outside. I used to sit with my sister in our wading pool and wonder what it would be like if it was in the middle of the living room. In Laurel and Hardy, pianos (bourgeois sanctities) end up in lily ponds; houses flood. Men camp in the attic. *Trespass* is a common form of excitement and sometimes it's purely physical objects that provide it.

There was an artist on the loose a few years back who specialized in invading people's houses when they weren't at home, rearranging their belongings into bizarre totem-like towers, sometimes even *flooding their rooms* and placing forbidding, taxidermied birds of prey atop the assemblages and photographing them – then disassembling everything and putting it back just as it had been before. Then he'd send the owners these pictures. As a Laurel and Hardy person, this made perfect sense to me. The only difference is that Laurel and Hardy were not usually able to rectify the damage done before their wives came home.

There are thrilling moments of social trespass in Laurel and Hardy, which really is a land of outlandish, nervous-making decorum: in *Blotto*, Hardy is so frustrated when he can't remember Laurel's telephone number that *he tears a page out of a public telephone book*, licks it, and sticks it to the wall of the drug store phone booth he's in. That gave me a very strange feeling. But this isn't vandalism, wanton destruction for its own sake – it's what happens when you finally lose your rag with your friend who's an idiot and there's no booze and the etiquette of the telephone is suddenly beyond you.

WHAT DID I KNOW about married life, night-clubs, tenors or even telegrams? But even though I knew nothing about seduction, employment, rich people, cars, angry cops, alcohol, nursemaids or pianos, I knew that Laurel and Hardy's neighborhood was only a few miles away. If I'd been allowed up on our roof, I might just have been able to glimpse them, on theirs.

About 1960 the brothers next door with World

War Two dangling from their ceiling moved away and these two new kids moved in. Their names were Artie (Arthur) and Gary. But when they came over to introduce themselves, with their baseball mitts, I thought that Artie had introduced himself as 'Hardy'. I could not believe my luck – I was going to live next door to guy named HARDY. I was on the brink of nirvana. So I was talking to them about the neighborhood and stuff and I kept saying to Gary, 'When you and Hardy want to do so-and-so . . .', and finally Gary interrupted with 'WHO'S *HARDY*?' I took this very badly. It turned out they were pretty militaristic too – every Fourth of July they sank a flotilla of sparkler-stuffed model boats in their swimming pool.

In the end there'll be nothing left, no movies, nothing electronic, so that *descriptions of movies in books* is all the saucer men will have access to. So here are the essential gags of *Blotto*.

Laurel wants to go out and have fun with Hardy in a nightclub. But Mrs. Laurel is playing solitaire and seems in a bad mood. Hardy telephones and Laurel is too frightened to speak to him in front of his wife. After calling Laurel several times, Hardy tells him to 'send himself a telegram' as a way of getting out of the house.

This Laurel does. He writes out a telegram blank, puts it in an envelope, *climbs out the window*, lodges the envelope on the front porch, rings his own door-bell, and climbs back through the window. Mrs.

Laurel, having listened in on the extension, knows just what he's up to. But she plays along with everything, fascinated to see to what lengths Laurel will go to get out of the house for the evening. So she tells him she thinks there's someone at the door.

Laurel starts to go but heads first for the window, catching himself just in time. (One of the genius aspects of Laurel's character is that things can only ever go right for him *for a few seconds*.) He goes out on the front porch and enacts a complicated, jovial exchange with the nonexistent Western Union boy, even pretending to tip him. He goes back inside, immediately returning to the porch as he's forgotten to pluck the fake telegram from its hiding place. And at this moment he looks at the camera and gives us a wonderful open-mouthed frown – a 'how could I be so stupid' look. That might have been the moment when he grabbed me forever. To be *included* in that way.

Laurel pretends to read the telegram and tells Mrs. Laurel he's been called away on important business. She's fuming but still going along with his duplicity. Laurel has designs on a bottle of whiskey she's been hiding and she dumps it out and refills it with cold tea, Tabasco and a lot of other icky stuff. When Laurel leaves, Mrs. Laurel pointedly says goodnight to Hardy, who's outside hiding behind a sickly bush. The hiding idea was very exciting – it was just as hard to hide on our block as on theirs.

Now we're in the nightclub. There are some good

21

gags with regard to opening their bottle surreptitiously – it's Prohibition. Laurel and Hardy have already attracted attention as they're underdressed – everyone else is in evening clothes. This makes you nervous from the start.

Laurel watches Hardy take the first drink of Mrs. Laurel's 'whiskey'. A truly alarming series of expressions and grimaces pass across Hardy's face and he finally says, 'You can certainly tell good liquor when you taste it!' They proceed to get drunk on this stuff.

A *tenor* arrives at their table and launches into a ballad of the most incredible bathos, 'The Curse of an Aching Heart'. Listening to this, Laurel becomes tipsily lachrymose. Hardy begins to be affected too and has impulses to comfort Laurel. By the end of the song Laurel is in morbid hysteria. Hardy offers the tenor a drink, and he spits it out. By now completely under the influence, *of nothing*, Laurel suddenly starts to find everything funny. This transformation from despair to hilarity in the space of about a minute is simply one of the great human documents. It shows just about everything we're capable of – or not. If you're ever stranded anywhere with no Beckett, watch *Blotto*.

What about Stan Laurel's crying arrested me? His on-the-edge-of-tears mode I adopted for myself and it really exasperated my parents. I probably still do some buried version of it when I am upset. I know I have. I've done some *stupid movie things* at wrong moments in my life. But why didn't I have my *own* way of crying? At that age, of course, one is always trying to discover the *effects* of things on a potential audience. But maybe this is something that everyone raised on cinema should ask: have I felt the need to incorporate these things into my own act? And why?

Laurel's laughing in *Blotto* is maybe the most he ever did on screen. Usually he looked sad – as sad as I felt.

Mrs. Laurel arrives in the nightclub with an extremely large gun. Hardy, who's been drawn into Laurel's imaginary alcoholic hilarity, is the first to see her and sobers instantly. He tries to get Laurel's attention. When Laurel eventually looks over and sees her, he thinks it's the funniest thing yet. He can barely breathe enough to be able to tell her that they stole the bottle, which he brandishes at her. She tells them it was only cold tea. At this Laurel sobers up.

Mrs. Laurel unwraps her gun and Laurel and Hardy flee – in the lobby Mrs. Laurel scatters the customers and check-room girls and sends a waiter and his glassware flying – Laurel and Hardy scramble into a taxi – as it starts down the street Mrs. Laurel emerges from the club and calmly takes aim – one blast of her shotgun (always these guns are very loud) reduces what was a taxi to a heap of flailing limbs, dust and scrap. Mrs. Laurel trots toward it with quite a seductive wiggle.

Gags

I was talking with an admirer of Laurel, a very funny man himself. He'd read that in the evenings, and on weekends, Laurel was always hard at work, inventing gags. *Can you believe that?* the guy said to me. *How could he do that?* I found it perplexing that this guy *couldn't* imagine it. What else would Stan Laurel be doing?

To be able to take a radio or a watering can or a St. Bernard and make it funny requires that you take the view that the world is incredibly hostile to us. And it is. So – you get depressed, and you write gags. Art is a gag.

There are some pens on the desk here. They could squirt me. They could poke me. One could roll off onto the chair and I could sit on it when I come back from making tea – I'd jump up yelling and upset everything on the desk and I'd have an indigo bottom and ink would get in the teapot and I'd have big indigo lips. Or I could absent-mindedly pick up the black pen, thinking it was a cigar, and light it – or I could reach out and take a cigar and try to write with it, burning a hole in this chapter. And my pants.

Some of the fun in sight gags comes from a *love of destruction* which is not very healthy, and these days it's way out of control: the only movies most people now attend are nothing more than a series of explosions. Cars, houses, children, women, men, dogs, cats, cities,

Russians and dinosaurs of all kinds all blown to bits in increasingly sadistic ways. Because we westerners, Americans in particular, hate and fear ourselves and the physical universe we have created. And we should. Laurel's revenge on us is to show *it* winning a lot of the time.

The Model T Ford was supposed to democratize travel. But for many it was like dealing with a mad beast. A radio is a benign device that brings culture into the home – until it is you yourself that has to go up on the roof and install the aerial.

PIANO + LONG FLIGHT OF STEPS = HELL.

What I want to know is, were there people in the world who *hated* to watch Oliver Hardy get his car sawn in half? *Oh, look at that, he shouldn't be doing that! What a waste!* Were there people who took it *amiss* that Stan Laurel and Oliver Hardy extravagantly tossed Christmas trees through windows in frustration? Because *my* gags often backfired.

My family. My family were funny – we used to laugh at a lot of the same things.

A family supper on the patio. It was summer. My grandparents were visiting and the table was crowded. Time for watermelon! I started to clear – I wanted to help and be efficient. I had in my arms lots of plates and saucers of what I thought of as our *picnic china*, just a lot of funny-looking old Spanish style china, I didn't even know where it had come from. Half way

across the patio it all started to slip. I knew immediately it was a lost cause and I *slumped*, at a certain
telling moment no longer attempting to save all the
plates, letting some of them slide slowly to the concrete
floor and break. I cast a very Buster Keaton look at my
grandmother and she cracked up. Truly: tremendous
laugh. My biggest laugh yet. She'd never seen anything
so funny.

Turned out this was her wedding china. Set out on
purpose for the occasion of her visit. Guess the gag was
on me! Some of those plates survived. They're in the
colors of 1920s California movie palaces, if you want
to get all blurry about it: gold, blue, red and orange.
They haunt me.

But my timing was perfect.

I wasn't totally enamored with just anything 'comic' –
the Keystone Kops, Chaplin, for instance, were lost on
me. I was a sophisticate. But I did have a short pie-in-
the-face period, inspired not by Mack Sennett or even
Laurel and Hardy's major expedition into custard (*The
Battle of the Century*) but by Soupy Sales, a kids' show
host who took a pie in the face every day.

They weren't real pies, with a crust that would
slowly slough off your face after you'd been hit (adding
to the joke) – they were merely piles of aerosol shaving
cream on paper plates.

I knew that paper plates were available (we were
picnickers) and that shaving cream could be purchased

in small cans. I began a campaign to obtain these materials and have a pie fight.

There were objections raised: expense. Waste. But these are the familiar, tiresome objections that must always be resisted and overcome by the artist. Eventually I wore my mother down on a trip to the supermarket and I had it – *I had the equipment.* Okay, I had wheedled and cringed, but she came through. WHAT A MOM. I called Fard and told him to come over. My mother wouldn't have wanted the neighbors to know she had condoned this and quickly disappeared from the whole scene after giving us two threadbare towels.

So we sprayed shaving cream on the plates and smacked each other with 'em, uttering hastily improvised witty lines, until the stuff was all gone, which was pretty quickly. Then a kind of lassitude descended on us. You need more, but you're not going to get any more. No applause. Loneliness . . . It suddenly felt 'cold', very cold for California. Fard went home.

WASTE? Throwing and receiving those pies was the greatest moment of my life so far. I can imagine my parents discussing it later the same evening. *Oh well, maybe he's got it out of his system . . .*

There was no concept of waste in Laurel and Hardy. You have to fake a trip to Hawaii? Bring home a pineapple. You need to move a piano? Spend the whole day lugging it up the longest flight of steps in Los Angeles. Aggravation is infinite.

What Is and Is Not Funny

The reason Fard and I enjoyed this stuff was that at the age of seven we understood comic timing. Children do, as it's the rhythm of life. Adults lose track of what a force it is. We'd taken this in subconsciously, but we could use it. I was perhaps unusual in studying this kind of comedy so closely, but of course the great source of humor for us was cartoons. All kinds of cartoons *poured* out of the television, most of them terrible, because they were made by men who didn't know what was funny (Walt Disney encouraged Mickey Mouse to torture other animals). There were cartoons so ancient, crude and dim that I can't remember who 'starred' in them. Bosco? Chucko? Jocko? Then the 1960s became the breeding ground of cartoons made for television, which had very limited animation, and no comic timing, except in the voice work.

But there were a few artists involved in cartoons – Max Fleischer, Tex Avery and Bob Clampett to name three – who raised the art of comic timing until it was absolutely perfect.

Daffy Duck Slept Here is a slightly surreal cartoon where Porky Pig has to share a hotel bed with Daffy Duck. There's a tussle over the sheets and a hint of bedwetting, each idea supplanted and bettered so quickly that it's breathtaking. The opera singer made to hold a note by Bugs Bunny (impersonating Stokowski) – the colors his face turns in rapid succession, including tartan. The classic Bugs/Daffy confrontation and a gem of dialogue writing, 'It's fiddler crab season!' And these were the cartoons we laughed at: the ones that were funny. Even as cinema cartoons were being destroyed by television, the Road Runner pictures proposed a newer, higher level of timing, and a return to silent film principles. The coyote's pupils shrinking as he turns to face an approaching locomotive – he's of course on the tracks in a shed full of TNT.

The tantrums of Donald Duck *can* be funny, though not as effectively as the neuroses of Daffy. Disney cartoons aren't funny. At Disney they wasted all their time and money on *capitalistic winsomeness.*

One night in the 1970s a quite decrepit movie theater somewhere in the West 20s advertised it was going to show every Laurel & Hardy film they could get their hands on, back-to-back. It was a real flophouse – very few of the smelly snoring men in it had any interest in Laurel and Hardy – they slept there every night. It was winter and the place was totally unheated. My friend Jim was laughing at some of the first few gags in *Big Business* and then he started to shiver, then shudder, then we both fell asleep from cold. I imagine I slept straight through some brilliant two-reelers that I'd never seen, or hadn't seen since the days of Commander Rip Tide. If only he could have spotted us in his periscope and rescued us. We were unconscious the whole night, aside from one horrifying trip to the toilet and what I found there and I couldn't feel my legs when we woke up and fled. The lost Laurel and Hardy classic: *Hypothermia*.

– Technicolor –

To describe Technicolor? Can you describe the simultaneous luxury and necessity of water? Of bread? Of your mother? Could you pin down, if asked, exactly what it feels like to get into a warm bath, knowing that your pajamas await? Or to wake up, warm and content, without care? Christmas, Hallowe'en, hearing that your friend is coming for a visit – do these have a taste, a special light surrounding them?

Talk about things you would never want to do without: the pictures in *The Bumper Book*, unsettling as they were (or, to give it its full name, *The Bumper Book of Unsettling Wicker Things and Small Mammals' Eyes*). The smell of outside in your town, industrial as it might have been. The aroma of your father's pipe. The exact taste of sugar cookies with red sprinkles – not a taste *something* like that. Lying in bed with an erection – the kind that won't do anything to you and you won't do anything to it. Money in the bank.

Seeing your cat come in the door and walk toward you with a smile on her face. Noticing that it is autumn. Being tucked in. Looking at a favorite Kodacolor snapshot. Staring at a rug or upholstery or the wallpaper until it opens up, invites you in. Smell of pine needles, the sound of a small, lone outboard motor on a summer lake. The feeling you get on a day in second grade when the girl whom you ever so slightly admire wears her calico dress.

Technicolor did things like this to you. The look of a campfire in a western. Of John Wayne's skin and his *beads of sweat*. Of dust, uniforms, headbands, hoe-downs. Pinks and blacks in musicals, skies that looked like the crazy, *stolen skies* on postcards. Doris Day's long, pale wool coats. Cary Grant's suit. Imagine the effect on the psyches of the grown-ups of the weird rainbow-colored silk-shaded window in Douglas Sirk's *All That Heaven Allows* – ! It's like an acid trip, MAN. He *freaked 'em out*. So much for Mr. and Mrs. Normal.

My wife thinks that synesthesia doesn't exist, that it's the dream stuff of fakeroos and they should shut up about it. But Technicolor was a kind of *forced synesthesia* – Vincente Minnelli and country roads and railroad stations that looked like music.

In a way it was a weapon, a weapon of mass distraction. We made many brutal cultural inroads on the world with Technicolor. Perhaps now we are paying the price. For sharing it and then for revoking it, as we did with so many things.

Technicolor didn't end on the flat plane of the screen. It bled out into the *décors* of the movie theater. Whether it was the Fox in our town or the Egyptian or the Chinese in Hollywood. Technicolor followed me around, in my day dreams and even in my dreams. I never thought of the girl in second grade that I ever so slightly admired in any other way. I made up songs about her, made up whole movies starring her on my way to school, movies with large juicy yellow titles.

Décors of the Theaters

A wavy red velvet that possibly had not been seen since the Renaissance, gold that had an equal effect. It was strange that our church had no red or gold, no deep colors in it at all, whereas going into the Fox was like stepping into *Robin Hood*. Our church was the most wan thing imaginable. The outside was stucco and maybe a little stone or artificial stone, and inside, the walls were plaster painted an enervating shade of Episcopalian gray or sick green, the altar made of fieldstone. Behind the pulpit was a wonky triangular window not of stained glass, just panels of several tints, including a yellow that always sickened me because it reminded me of the heavy yellow tumblers of water you got in unpleasant coffee shops where the lamps were wagon wheels and the booths were sticky and too big for you. Enough! Let's just say it was a *Natalie Kalmus church*.

Technicolor saturated us. It was somewhat dis-admired for that – in some quarters it was a term of disparagement, like 'saccharine' or 'Disney'. But satu-ration was its hypnotic quality; how it conquered the world. Natalie Kalmus, wife of the founder of Technicolor and for many years the mandated color 'advisor' on any movie using the process, spent her career *trying to tone Technicolor down*. She was always trying to get the sets dressed in gray, which can be very effective – look at *White Christmas*. But most producers and directors in the Fifties and Sixties were looking for something *blinding*, and they thought Mrs. Kalmus was a crank. That the Kalmi had a famously unhappy marriage might account for some of her desire to MUTE, to muffle her husband's vibrant invention. With people of my generation Technicolor is a point of view that we will always have, to which we will always be able to appeal.

After he finished his engineering degree in 1950, the first job interview my father had was at Technicolor. Once he saw what I was becoming, he wisely kept this from me for many years. BUT WE COULDA BEEN IN THE MOVIE BUSINESS!

Occasionally we were taken to Hollywood, not to a premiere but to a big movie recently opened. Hollywood Boulevard always looked plain to me – it looked like the main street in our town except a little wider – otherwise it was drug stores and these depressing Southern California furniture stores. Lots of pine, fake colonial, disturbing fabrics of rust brown with metallic threads running through.

I never wanted to go to Grauman's Chinese Theater, I wanted to go to the *Egyptian* Theater, because I was mad on Tutankhamun. But still, the Egyptian Theater *was nowhere near Egyptian enough*, in my opinion. It looked more Babylonian or Mesopotamian in its volumes, but who's going to say *Hey, let's catch a flick at the Mesopotamian*? How do you go about designing an Egyptian popcorn stand? Well, they did it.

In the courtyard of the Chinese Theater they had the hand and foot prints of the stars, the American equivalent of getting yourself buried in Westminster Abbey. I thought it was pretty underwhelming since I'd never heard of most of these people. And Laurel and Hardy had never even been invited! This forecourt had a forlorn quality, like the cement was wearing away or they didn't hose it off enough. Were there leaves blowing around? Trash?

The amusing thing is that the Chinese Theater usually had the better movies. I remember being taken to some kid nonsense at the Egyptian, it might have been *Hans Christian Andersen* with Danny Kaye, or *The Wonderful World of the Brothers Grimm*. I came to dread expeditions to Hollywood for this kind of giant goddamn kid nonsense. The further you went for this stuff, the worse it always was, plus there was the disappointment of watching something truly awful in a movie *palace*.

Danny Kaye reminds me of a disrespectful song a friend of mine used to sing about a distributor of

16mm films, to the tune of 'Wonderful, Wonderful Copenhagen':

> *Wonderful, wonderful Audio Brandon,*
> *They'll sell you films by the ton –*
> *With the splices in, and the air-holes in . . .*

It might, on the other hand, have been some pan-familial stuff like *Around the World in 80 Days*. O it was colourful all right, but to the Vernophile it was just a monster series of bullfights and OOGA BOOGA, like stereo LP exotica of the time.

So here you have all this stereo and Cinemascope and Cinerama (phewww – what a flop) and Techni-color and you use it, ultimately, to *push the world away* from America, to make it ridiculous and unreal. Pretty funny, but that's what we did. *That's what we all did.*

Since we're talking exhibitors, I can now reveal that when she was in college my mother dated a guy whose family owned some movie theaters. He liked her a lot – this is the family legend. (He had nothing on my dad, though, who had a pipe and his own skis.)

My mother kept this from us for many years. WE COULDA BEEN IN THE MOVIE BUSINESS!

The Fox Fullerton

There was a broad marquee and underneath it a box office. The marquee sported a neon sign – *Fox*, in swash

– and chase lights. Under the marquee, you could wait in case of rain – ha! – if you looked up, there were dim bulbs in white recesses surrounded by gold, set in a sky blue ground. I can remember this because when we went to the Fox Theater my brain was on RED ALERT. In the box office was a machine that smoothly spat tickets at you with a kind of *harrumph, harrumph* from a perfectly flat steel plate. Then we walked through a little courtyard which was the norm in California movie theaters of the Spanish style. You went inside and there was the damp tearing sound when you gave your ticket to the sallow man with the Tall Thing, a specially-designed metal box for receiving the tickets you'd just bought twenty seconds before – every time I wished the tickets made a crisper noise. Although for 25¢ . . . The smell of popcorn, cigarettes, the *smell of heavy carpeting.* I remember thinking that the Fox was a clean place, though it probably wasn't. In the auditorium were two chief pleasures, the Big Chandelier which had hundreds of bulbs in it, and the Big Curtain.

The Fox Theater was one of the two places where I felt comfortable. Our living room sofa was the other one. In the Fox Theater I saw such elevating woiks o art as *The Absent-Minded Professor.* In a movie theater that you love, it doesn't matter what you watch. Once for some unknown reason, except perhaps that she was a real lady, our mother treated us to heavily upholstered loge seats. The idea seemed to be that if you were going to be this far from the screen, at least you ought to be comfortable. It was *Babes in Toyland*, the Disney one, and we couldn't make head or tail of it.

Budding Projectionist

Once after the lights came up my father took me down to the front, to examine the screen itself. He showed me that the surface was very rough, with millions of heavy glass beads. *These screens are very expensive*, he said. *That's why it's bad to throw soda and popcorn at them.* This added to my wonderments about the place where *he* grew up.

When I was seven, I was going to be an Egyptologist, the skipper of a submarine, or a projectionist, which would have in some ways incorporated the other two: a projectionist unlocks certain aesthetic mysteries, and he also has at his command a lot of valves, switches, levers and bells. And there's a bonus, as for a motion picture projectionist the possibility of being crushed to death on the floor of the sea or dying in agony from an ancient curse is somewhat reduced.

I'm not sure why I asked my father to take me to the projection room (perhaps my attraction to machinery combined with my love of what was hidden), but I made him do it a lot.

This quivering, blinking muscle of light in a cinema – it's been written about hundreds of times, shown fondly in hundreds of movies – we all respond to it. We find ourselves watching the beam instead of the picture. The queer thing is that it no longer exists, because nobody smokes. Whatever the health implications, it's an aesthetic pity. We'll just have to imagine that we sense it, feel it, in future – like unprotected sex.

We would go up dim stairs no longer used by the public, carpeted in the Thirties maybe – sometimes we had to go outside the building on long scary catwalks (older projection rooms were architecturally separate from the auditorium because of the fire risk of nitrate film).

An impressive heat in a projection room – big smooth levers for changing over from one projector to another – warning bells that clanged just like aboard the *Nautilus*. Dimly lit dials, ditto.

These men, what were they? Witch doctors? Ministers of a kind? Did they remember every scene they had watched two hundred times? I was impressed by anyone who did complicated stuff smoothly – bakery wagon doughnut men, cable car gripmen, projectionists . . . They had a peculiar esthetic power – there was an artistry to projection. It used to take five years to learn. That's the kind of information that can drive your parents insane, that you might spend five years of the life they gave you learning how to open and close a curtain and throw some switches. But if a thing is worth doing . . . And at least it's show business.

At the Cinema Village in New York, they used to buy used carbon elements from the bigger theaters uptown. Therefore the screen often went black in the middle of the picture as these cheapo carbons burned out. Time and again the patrons would hoot, run up the aisle waving their fists . . . people got really mad when they were suddenly deprived of the *beam*.

These days I partake of Technicolor as if it is a food. Which it is. On Sunday afternoons we go to the market near our house and buy a pie or a chicken and a bottle of wine. We come home and have our lunch and then it's time for Technicolor! It no longer matters what the picture is, not one bit. Technicolor sends me into a dwalm – I'm fond of *To Catch a Thief* in this way, although I've never seen the end of it. The Technicolor puts me to sleep. *The Trouble with Harry* is the same. It's full of glorious, outrageous fake New England fall foliage. Even James Bond will occasionally do (as long as it has some ocean in it), or a non-annoying musical, if it is day on which I am thinking that musicals are not annoying.

One might chew, slurp and snore one's way through *The Birds* (some of the perfect colors of California), *Singin' in the Rain* particularly for *that* rain, *An American in Paris* for the fake Paris streets in Hollywood sunlight. Even Disney's *Kidnapped* has done for my Technicolor dessert. But if I really want to secure my disaffection from society in this way for well over two hours, there's always *It's a Mad, Mad, Mad, Mad World*, a hugely flawed epic comedy that really dishes up the color – and it was in Cinerama.

And then there is Sirk. As a child in the Fifties I was unaware of Douglas Sirk and his devastating, subversive use of Technicolor. But I realize now that I was *living* the life, that I was a victim of the life that he was blisteringly illustrating. For most others Technicolor was a way of mesmerizing the crowd in order to entertain it. Sirk used it like a medical laser. Take a look at that window in the daughter's bedroom in *All That Heaven Allows* – the acid-trip light that it emanates, as the family starts to disintegrate.

I occasionally thrill to his more muted scenes, too – there's a particular medical register to his palette – operating gowns of light gray, pale green walls, anesthetic masks of black and red rubber seem to sum up every medical experience of the 1950s, every glimpse one had of a hospital. (These same medical colors appear in Nicholas Ray's *Bigger Than Life* – you can feel the big iron hypodermic needles and smell the mercurochrome.)

It's true that there's a lot of black and white that's as luscious as Technicolor: the deep blacks in *42nd Street*, the richness of the cigarette-lighting scenes in *Now, Voyager*, the scenes on the moors in *The 39 Steps*. I was going to say something here about *British* color, its plainer qualities, and so on, but British color is more a contradiction in terms, sometimes like the idea *British movie* is in general. I pity them.

The more intellectual way you can spend Sundays is in watching movies about New York: *The Apartment, All About Eve, Holiday* . . . Some New York movies also supply a Technicolor fix: *When Harry Met Sally, Desk Set, Bell Book and Candle, North by Northwest, The Hudsucker Proxy.* Sometimes I think I'd prefer to spend eternity watching movies about people working in offices in New York. *I'd* be lying down, naturally.

Re-enactment

Every year they showed *The Wizard of Oz* on tel-evision. Sometimes it was around Thanksgiving and sometimes around Easter. I don't want to bore you . . . the movie itself isn't boring, of course, it's often charming and exciting and unfortunately all too fas-cinating for millions, billions of people whose lives it's practically ruined, good gods the stuff that has been written about it, read into it, grave-robbed about it. The Judy Garland ghouls, the munchkin websites, the shoe fetishists descending on Sotheby's to bid against each other for the ruby slippers . . . *The Wizard of Oz* has a hold on trillions of people that they can't under-stand or even acknowledge. It's an inherent national weakness. (Maybe it's the great American novel. That would be sad. But many are riveted and even guided by *The Wizard of Oz* in a way they aren't by Fitzgerald or Hemingway.)

We were driven to a fever pitch by this thing. After

watching it we had to talk about it and we couldn't sleep because the next day we knew it would really be *ours*. The next morning everyone under the age of fifteen on our street woke early, bolted their Frosted Flakes and hurried outside, kids streaming into the street, to ASSEMBLE, the right of the kids peaceably to assemble! So that we could re-enact *The Wizard of Oz*.

If it had been shown at Easter, sometimes we ran out of our houses immediately after the broadcast – it was bright and hot there – seventy-five degrees Fahrenheit on a spring evening, all you movie fans of the cold nations. We stood and looked at each other, especially my sister and I and Peggy Ditti and Becky Rogers and so on – we'd look up and down the street and work it into our heads, where the Yellow Brick Road was, where the forest. We might sketch one or two preliminary scenes, but we knew the big re-enactment would be the next day.

I can clearly picture the look of really hard thought on everyone's face. They never looked that way at school. Naturally. Our need was very urgent. Or like we were bees or something. Evolutionarily driven.

The neighborhood was our blank canvas, but it has to be said that it took a lot of imagination to make it into the locales of that picture. We were successful at squinting our eyes and telling ourselves we were in the same world as *Our Gang* – they too had been shot in Culver City, though their pictures had a much more countrified feeling than Laurel and Hardy's. The only thing that seemed rural about our neighborhood, aside from the rare vacant lot, was the culverts, large concrete drainage ditches we weren't allowed to go near because of the (extremely remote) danger of 'flash floods'. And we didn't *inhabit* our patch the way the kids in *Our Gang* did: they had *wherewithal* and they had *gadgets*. How we longed for the gadgets and little vehicles, their perfect contraptions, putatively made by Alfalfa and Spanky, but in reality they could only have been built by the cleverest Hollywood prop men. The kids in *Our Gang* didn't have to bother with many adults, except for the pretty schoolteacher Miss Crabtree, who was nice to them – Miss Crabtree who looks so much like my wife that I sometimes wake up in the night, frightened that Miss Crabtree is in the bed. They also had real autonomy, which is what we yearned for in our endless needs to reimagine Balfour Avenue as the Emerald City.

We moved like zombies through the story – I wish some parent had captured this on 8mm Kodachrome – but in truth I don't think any of our parents were ever aware of what we did once we went outside. So safe it all was. We weren't friends. We were *playmates*. We didn't know each other very well. I knew Fard, but he lived three streets down and he was never part of this our Oberammergau. Nonetheless we had unwritten, unspoken rules, huge rules for the re-enactment. The one thing that really upset us was when somebody didn't '*play right*'. You were PNG if you couldn't stick to the thing, meaning you failed to imagine it, remember it properly. One year Billy Turley excitedly suggested that the scenario should include 'moon martians', and he got the shit kicked out of him. The rules were *tough*. No genre-bending.

We didn't really care who played Dorothy or the Tin Man – we *were* the story *collectively*, as we moved through the neighborhood like army ants.

What we found most mysterious in the movie was the wizard's lair, the throne room, which was a nice piece of movie-making because it doesn't make any sense spatially and it's full of things that are hard to rationalize or describe – it's the most dream-like scene in Dorothy's dream that is the story. The throne room has some large glowing green plinths, a curious pillar, and a dais on which there are flame pots, the 'throne', and a curtain onto which the head of the wizard is projected. It's completely dark except for these garishly illuminated elements. When the wizard speaks, balls of fire erupt from the basins flanking the throne. (How did he build all this without the people of Oz knowing his secrets? After watching *The Egyptian*, I decided that he must have *killed* them all, like the Pharaoh did to all the guys who built the secret parts of his pyramid.)

How do you turn the inside of Becky Rogers's parents' garage into something like that? How does one thing become another? This is something that is often achieved in childhood. Becky's parents both had their cars out during the day so it was the most cavernous of the garages. We tried flashing the lights on and off, but. We hungered for the elaborate and violent special effects that had been mysteriously and enthrallingly achieved (only several miles from where we were gathered and only a few years before).

One Christmas I was given a flashlight that could be made to shine red or green. I brought this along and there was some approval. Another time I found an old automobile distributor cap somewhere and was shocked to discover that if I held it up close to my eye it looked almost exactly like the battlements of the castle of the Wicked Witch of the West. Do you see where things were going? Shouldn't we have been learning how to surf, or doing our homework? I was too embarrassed to tell anyone about the special properties of the distributor cap.

Peggy Ditti was sort of the line manager of these attempts for a while. She was wilful and imperious, and she was big so we followed her around. To my amazement she once wrote her name on a wall in my house with a crayon. She was impatient and unsatisfied with Becky Rogers's garage in the end. After several frustrating years I think that we all knew we weren't going to achieve any of this noise and fire and colour – and that the journey was the important thing and not to get bogged down in details, even though the details were what we thirsted for.

There were quite a few stands of bamboo in our neighborhood – some large enough to crawl into – and I suggested that they were green like the Emerald City and that we could stand near them, the sunlight behind, when we needed to be 'there'. This was agreed upon. And after a hard day of re-enactment I could take my distributor cap into the bath and hold it right up to my eyeball. In a good year we came close.

However I made a discovery I couldn't share. One summer evening my dad asked me to extinguish the barbecue, as he put the hot dogs and hamburgers on a platter, straightened his IT'S A MAN'S WORLD apron and headed for the kitchen. This meant getting the garden hose and dousing the glowing charcoal – it made a calamitous hissing noise and clouds of vapor and ash rose straight up in a column – just like the billowing clouds of smoke and fire in the throne room and I, I was the master of it. I liked to imagine what my head looked like behind all this steam . . . But we couldn't have gone around lighting and dousing barbecues for the re-enactments, so this had to be something for my head alone. Like the distributor cap.

I find it almost impossible to admit that we spent hours, perhaps hundreds of hours of our lives doing this. Yet such was the vastness of our mania and our leisure.

– *20,000 Leagues Under the Sea* –

T his is the kind of thing that happened to you if you grew up in the 1950s: you were turned into an enemy agent, acting against your own family, by the manufacturers of Robot Commando and Frosted Flakes. They fed you with endless movie and comic book versions of the world war that had just ended. And you got what Rossini you could from Bugs Bunny.

We frequented the public library in the next town, because it had a charming room just for children, complete with murals and tile pictures round a fireplace. As a Californian kid I always took an interest in fireplaces because I didn't know what they were for. In this library I discovered an illustrated book based on the Walt Disney movie of *20,000 Leagues Under the Sea*. So for a while the central text of my existence was an abridged and otherwise distorted, and *drawn*, version of a motion picture adaptation of a novel. We should call the Fifties the Age of Adaptation – did a single one of us experience the original of anything?

O, I was a submerged little fellow, submerged by worry – *adult* worries. THE BOMB – these frightening *drills* at school. When you're a boy and you think no one likes you, you get submerged in antagonism too. Boys are apt to want REVENGE – it's a very popular idea. Girls just go quietly insane. But this submergence in your own submergence, this is the very idea of Captain Nemo, whose very motto,

MOBILIS IN MOBILI

moving in the moving element, showed his original and vengeful power, his love of freedom. This is not so different from James Bond stuff (from which my parents always protected me) – Ian Fleming probably owes Jules Verne a lot – but Bond is extremely adolescent, the good guys *and* the bad guys. To have a CONTROL PANEL from which you can wreak havoc on everybody that annoys you in seventh grade – that is what James Bond is about. Can you imagine what an insipid, leering old drunk Ian Fleming must have been? What a *namby-pamby*? I keep him on the same detestable shelf in my mind as Tolkien, the shelf of really fouled-up English people who unleashed torrents of bullshit on the world from which we will never recover.

Yes, okay – of course there's some kind of *phallus trouble* going on when you build a cigar-shaped boat with a spike on the end of it and RAM other ships. But Captain Nemo did it in a good way. He was making war on war. If you have a splendid logically twisted idea like that you just have to run with it. At least in the movies. And of course we got it, on some level, that James Mason was having some kind of Weirdo

Orgasm when he called to the engine room for Collision Speed.

My father noted my interest in this story and one summer afternoon he began to read to me *Twenty Thousand Leagues Under the Sea. By Jules Verne*! We were in the 'breezeway' between the house and the garage; I think he was smoking a cigar. My excitement at finally getting *the real shit* cooled pretty rapidly under the tedious lecture on marine flora and fauna of which *Twenty Thousand Leagues Under the Sea* largely consists. My mouth was probably hanging open. My father, though sympathetic to my disappointments, carried on reading.

Several years before I could see the Disney picture, I had clocked a poster at the movies that said *20,000 Leagues* . . . ? But I couldn't understand why there was a curvy blonde lady pictured on this iron stairway – I started to vibrate and jump up and down and *point* . . . My dad came over and looked at it and said, rather sadly, 'Oh, that says twenty thousand *laughs* under the sea.' It was one of those post war comedies that everyone in the services hated because being in the military wasn't very funny. We were both very insulted. And what movie with a bunch of guys in T-shirts could possibly have even *twenty* laughs in it? What a GYP – coincidentally, this was a word I had learned from my dad on a bad little fake submarine ride at Pacific Ocean Park.

I was given a View-Master around this time, into which you put wheels of transparencies. Many sets of these were available with stereo vision of fairy tales, cartoons and so on. I had two picture sets. The first was travel photos of the Soviet Union, which had a picture of a beach resort on the Black Sea – there was a tubby unshaven man in a tiny black bathing suit scowling at the camera who scared me. But whether it was his blue face, tiny thong or the beach, which was composed of *rocks*, I don't know. The other set of pictures was *20,000 Leagues Under the Sea*, photographs of flexible dolls in little scenarios. They all had thick legs and looked deformed, really – the submarine wasn't right, it kept *changing*, and the 'giant octopus' looked like a watermelon. I almost puked. It probably *was* a watermelon.

To add to my *20,000 Leagues* frustrations, the sets built for the Disney film were at that time permanently on display at Disneyland, which I always insisted on seeing (we went there a lot). So I'd read the Disney illustrated book, choked on Jules Verne, *heard* about the movie, internalized the View-Master version, seen the model boats and had actually stood inside the *Nautilus*, as it were, in the luxurious salon, and gazed out the porthole at the giant squid and its snapping beak. But I still hadn't seen the movie. I was about to blow.

When I was around seven, Disney re-released *20,000 Leagues Under the Sea*. It was playing in some corner of our county – my father must have seen a little ad in the paper and shared this dangerous information with me. He could have kept it hidden from me for many years. He must have known this would immediately turn me into a pressure cooker, that there would be *no handling the kid* until he had seen the movie. My mother, the greatest enemy Walt Disney ever had, grudgingly decided that it was all right for me to see this – how could he wreck *that* after all? Of course he did wreck it, but in the rather surprising way of bolstering Nemo's role as anti-hero. The more you think about it, Disney's Nemo was really Disney – an inventive, angry, lonely fascist who loved machinery and rage, and brooked nothing from any *other* individualists. Bitter as shit. We brought Fard.

The streets of our county and even the interior of our car seemed totally unfamiliar; the ordinary little movie theater that we approached *could not possibly contain 20,000 Leagues Under the Sea!*

Many have written of the arresting images in this picture, particularly of the first sight of the *Nautilus* rushing at the American warship, glowing underwater, malevolent green. But no one was ever more excited about it than Fard and I were. Thrilling to the Todd-Fard imagination was particularly the operation of the *Nautilus* – all faintly illuminated nineteenth-century dials, levers, bells, hisses. They'd done their homework at Disney for once, you've got to give them that. (Of course, we expected Kirk Douglas's musical number (!) to be interrupted by *extreme violence . . .*).

Here we were, at last we were *really seeing it* –
Captain Nemo destroying warships. I was so excited I
was almost blind to it. And was he not the classiest kind
of bad guy? He collects ART. He lights the Professor's
(seaweed) cigar with a candle softly glowing in a
beautiful shell.

Someday they'll understand me! thought Todd
and Fard sitting together in the dark, thinking of the
horrors we were enduring in *elementary school*. James
Mason started this whole bad-guy-in-a-turtleneck
esthetic. Ever since this movie, smart bad guys have
taunted heroes while wearing smoking jackets and so
on – a kind of *déshabille* which suggests they never
have to go to an office, or even outside. They have
esthetic sensibilities, and probably girls tied up in the
back. They use a lot of big words and are promoters of
WEIRD FOOD (let a Frenchman loose in the ocean
. . . !). Great. It's all there. They make use of stuff.

CANNIBALS attack the *Nautilus* because Kirk
Douglas and Peter Lorre have set foot on their beach.
These 'natives' were way over the top, a bit OOGA
BOOGA. Their look I knew well from 'Adventureland'
– the iconography of their shields and so on was pure
Disney – I was also familiar with this kind of thing
from 'The Palms', a restaurant we often visited as a
family. It was 'Polynesian', pure 'TIKI', surrounded
by gardens with peacocks, and amongst the tribal
masks and bamboo and canoes there was a mynah
bird. That your parents could so casually throw out

the information that a mynah 'is a bird that talks' totally threw me. What this all meant, in the smoggy hodgepodge of Southern California, was that we were all capable of eating everything up. But I always drew the line at fish – I'd have been an unacceptable guest on the *Nautilus*. 'The sea would have had me back.'

Captain Nemo waits till there are quite a few cannibals on the deck of the *Nautilus* and then he electrifies the hull and they all jump around, all these underpaid black men, in a way that is not very comfortable to watch. But I'll bet it got a big laugh in 1954.

There's something disheartening, which I only noticed as an adult. When the cannibals climb onto the *Nautilus* from their swift and colorful outriggers, they creep along the deck towards the open hatch. One of them reaches out to one of the submarine's sturgeon-like iron fins, to steady himself, and it *wobbles*. Because there really was no *Nautilus* and this was just a wooden dummy anchored somewhere in the Bahamas on a sunny day in 1953. If I'd seen that floppy fin *that night*, with Fard, I don't know what . . . Life would have been very different. Perhaps impossible.

In the most famous sequence in the picture, the crew of the *Nautilus* battles a giant squid, another rather phallic customer, who's ensnared the boat. This squid, which was just a big marionette, was tricky. They were supposed to shoot a dramatic gory sunset fight scene, but the wires kept showing. They called up Walt himself. He came down to the set, took one look, and said something like *Shoot it at night, you jerks*. But my wife prefers the *sunset* squid (also available). 'Look at that,' she said, 'that's some real *vagina dentata*.'

Fard and I were Fifties kids, we were used to monsters. But see what we liked about this squid was that it was NEUROTIC, not HEROIC – neurotic in the extreme. This big archaic, antediluvian penis wanted to DRAG YOU DOWN, into the depths of your miserable pre-adolescent submergence, and you had to use this other big modern mechanical electrified penis to fight it. Simple.

Kirk Douglas betrays Captain Nemo, who gets shot in the end by a lot of Kiplingesque soldiers swarming his secret base. This was dramatic to the Todd and Fard mind – Nemo has just piloted the *Nautilus* with exquisite delicate skill through its hidden tunnel, and set up a time bomb so that the forces of the governments who hate him will never benefit from his inventions. The Kiplingesque soldiers shoot him just as he's descending back into the submarine – he takes the helm though and as he blearily steers the *Nautilus* back through the tunnel, crashing into rocks, you realize he's had it. They *had* to have James Mason to do this mortally wounded agony stuff – he does a version of it in almost every picture he's in – even in *North by Northwest* when he socks Martin Landau in the jaw.

And in *Bigger Than Life* he lays it on with a trowel. James Mason in pain.

Captain Nemo's was the first death I fully absorbed, unlike the stupid number of cavalry guys on television grabbing their chests and falling off their horses. And a lot of moths I put in jars. When you're an adult, all your plans can just end very quickly.

By the time we got home we had such *Nautilus boners* that we couldn't eat or think. We had to discuss the picture of course (Fard was staying over, natch) and we had to think how it could be re-enacted, which is what we did with everything – it was a psychological necessity. But the idea of the *Nautilus* was scrambling our brains. I lay in bed, carrying on a rambling, mumbling discussion with Fard. I remember saying that it was too bad that neither of our houses had a round window in it, so that we could stand at it and pretend it was the hemispherical porthole of the *Nautilus*'s wheelhouse, or even the big window in the salon, through which many wonders are witnessed by Paul Lukas, Peter Lorre and Kirk Douglas – this window frames the adventure. (When we played outer space, we would stand at the window in my room, or Fard's room – that would be Mission Control, and for headsets we held to our ears the sprayers from bottles of Windex. We never pretended *to be astronauts*, in a capsule, orbiting . . . we were only interested in *being in control*. This is what you saw on TV of course, all the guys with horn rims and white shirts and narrow ties. You hardly ever saw the astronauts, who seemed dim-witted and puffy.)

Nobody had round windows in our whole town, that was for sure.

Then, there in the night I made a miraculous discovery. My sister and I had a certain kind of night light in our rooms – they were flat white disks which, when plugged into the socket, glowed a soft turquoise blue. Round, it was round! I got out of bed and went and stuck my eye right on this thing. I zoomed in on it. It was a perfect porthole on a bright open sea, just a few feet below the surface. I woke Fard up and made him do it. He was impressed, though he pointed out the inconvenience of crawling across the floor to the electrical socket every time you had to be on the *Nautilus*. But it worked for me – any time I wanted I could gaze out of one of the portholes of the *Nautilus*, and it was the only thing that was going to satisfy a *Nautilus* boner. The next day we went to the hardware store and got Fard the identical night light for sticking his eye next to.

When Captain Nemo is dying, he asks Professor Aronnax if he knows what love is. Aronnax says he thinks he does. Captain Nemo says, 'What you fail to understand is the power of hate. It can fill the heart as fully as love can.' This is what every disaffected, submerged little boy has thought, through the ages.

You could make a flag out of it. Some have.

About 1973 I actually said this, to a girl who was breaking up with me. I think she liked me, but I bet that she knew she couldn't rescue me from my submergence. From my submarine, really, in which I was still vengefully traversing the world. I really have no idea why I said it, but I did. It was just the most dramatic thing that was handy. So this was another one of the stupid movie things I have done, like dropping Grandma's plates on the concrete.

— Hulot —

We had this way of taking vacations. They would put us in the car and drive 125,000 miles without stopping and then we would get out and be stunned to find ourselves somewhere weird. We hadn't taken in anything of the landscape along the way because we were too short to see out of the car. This in itself seems a Jacques Tati-esque position to be in, that you would be but the slightest suggestion of a head, the top of a sphere just rising above the rim of an automobile window.

Around 1958 they did this and we landed in Missoula, Montana, the town where my father had grown up. To me, at age five, the trip had been a kaleidoscope of primitive moteliana: log cabin walls, toilet seats guarded by paper strips with pictures of nurses' heads printed on them, the unchanging smell of cigarette smoke saturating the popcorn bedspreads. The surprise of an open fire at night. I did notice the weather changing: I'd never really been 'cold' before. Perhaps I'd felt 'cold' after a day at the swimming pool, but shit it was still 85°F out!

Missoula seemed a place of muted colours. My grandparents' house was what anyone would have expected then – white, surrounded by some trees. My grandmother cooked large breakfasts and in the basement my grandfather made small objects out of wood.

As a young and chauvinistic Californian I was surprised to find that Missoula had a freeway with an overpass – I thought all that malarkey was the privilege and doom of Angelenos exclusively. We travelled on this small freeway (maybe it was only a busy bridge) to go to the movies one afternoon, visiting relations being what it is.

I can't remember the cinema we visited (it might have been the Wilma or the Fox), or whether I demanded to be taken to the projectionist. I must have been intimidated by the place in some way. But what happened in that movie theater has endured with me: *Mon Oncle.*

Perhaps it's poetic to couch my memory of this in terms of *coats*, but of course to me this made the whole occasion memorable – it was 'cold' and we had to put on coats to get in the car and then wear our coats into the cinema which was full of people – grown-ups – all wearing coats and all *laughing.* I had never been in the company of so many adults laughing, laughing like *children.*

The way they were laughing, these people whom I hadn't expected to be like us, or like me – and that they were laughing at something from *Europe.* When was the last time Americans appreciated anything that isn't American? Maybe that *was* the last time – that very day! It's been a while, anyway. And I'm not talking about all the phonies who go to China and gush about it.

The Missoulians were laughing, of course, at the Arpels' modernistic fish fountain in their tiny paved front yard, its spasmodic strangling gurgles as it's switched on or off according to the status of who's at the front gate. Also the higgledy-piggledy house Hulot himself lives in, in 'Old Paris'. The maze of stepping-stones in front of the would-be minimalist, 'simple' house of the Arpels and the two round windows that become suspicious eyes at night when Monsieur and Madame Arpel peer out, as Hulot attacks their espaliered fruit tree. They were laughing at the housemaid being too afraid to step into the beam of the electric eye, and at Hulot's exploration of his sister's ultra-modern kitchen, the baffling appliances which force him to destroy things. Above all they laughed at the terrier under a table at the market in the old square, who bares his teeth and snarls menacingly at the big fish protruding from Hulot's shopping bag.

Tati's gags have a lot to do with aspirations: to be successful, to be accepted, loved. To be good. We are going to be thwarted in these, more than somewhat, as Damon Runyon would say. The physical world itself suggests this and Tati set himself to demonstrate it for us. (Everyone who leaves the Arpels' garden party has been smirched or injured in some way.)

Tati shows us how comedy is happening to us all the time – it's not just a 'take' on the world, it's *there*. It's occurring to you today, the same way you're being bombarded by cosmic rays. In fact, for some, this might be a grim realization. But it's unavoidably the truth. Tati said, 'The whole world is funny.'

Tati is more than a dream landscape. To me it's about an actually realizable world.

There is nothing better than Tati. Bach maybe.

So here was a live action beautifully colorful picture with sight (and sound) gags and timing equal or superior to that of any cartoon. And the grownups were loving it! Tati was teaching us Americans a little something, a modest lesson in what might be lost in modernity.

In *Mon Oncle* there was a whole new visual element for me to take in, and that was Europe. In Europe kids wore uniforms to school, bicycle tires were gray, and everything looked at once orderly and various, like the wooden 'city' I had that came in a box. Small, too, and cramped, compared to what was roaring all around us.

Last year I was on a bus in Edinburgh, which contains many, many buses. Across from me were a little American boy and his father. The kid had obviously been struck by how many buses there were and had been counting them: 'Ninety-six, ninety-seven, ninety-eight,' he went, 'one hundred! A hundred buses, Dad! What kind of a crazy country is this, anyway?'

Mon Oncle is decidedly 'modern' and 'European'-looking: the Arpels' house, much as it's supposed to be an esthetic warning on the way things are going in society, still possesses a lot of French charm.

Some of the great moments in the picture are about the totally unusable furniture of the future: the sofa consisting of three long cylinders that causes the neighbor to emit a little shriek when she sits on it; the unworkably tiny cafe table with parasol where M. Arpel takes his coffee; the kidney-shaped divan that Hulot can only sleep on by turning it on its side, his shoes, stripy socks and pipe strewn on the living room floor to the horror of his sister. (*Viz.* Woody Allen trying to sit on a futuristic 'chair' made only of a thin strip of metal in *Sleeper.*)

These days we are all trying our damnedest to be 'modern', struggling to get to grips with the increasing amount of technology rammed down our throats. We're losing. Steve Jobs is making fools of us from beyond the grave. As surely as the automatic kitchen in *Mon Oncle* got the better of Hulot. His best efforts at the brother-in-law's factory result in plastic sausages.

We kids of the Fifties were struggling with what it meant to be modern in our own way: A-bomb drills aside, there was the space race, which made everyone paranoid. When you went to Disneyland, for what good that did you, you could take a trip to the moon. But more interesting to me, there was a modern house to visit, the Monsanto House of the Future.

(Yes: Monsanto, the world's biggest pest, had a poison tendril in our childhood.) The thing that impressed me the most about this house of the future was that there was a TELEVISION built into the wall of the KITCHEN! And now that's the thing that *de*presses me most: the ubiquity of screens.

Nowadays there's no interest in the future, satirical or otherwise, because we're all doomed. And the IT guys know that.

There were two Warner Brothers cartoons involving modern appliances and futuristic houses that frightened me a lot. The cartoons are funny but they're also sadistic, in the way of Chaplin. One is *Dog Gone Modern*, from 1939, in which a pair of dogs get into a 'model home' that is wired to do everything, and quickly run afoul of these devices (even though the house features an 'Automatic Dog Bone Dispenser'). There's an electric-eye joke at the beginning not dissimilar to that in *Mon Oncle*. The look of these machines is impersonal. They're like Alexander Calder pieces only hostile. That the robots have small spheres instead of heads really spooked me.

One of the key gags is that the first dog keeps getting snagged by the automatic dishwashing device, pulled into the sink and remorselessly scrubbed. (It's rather like Chaplin's automatic eating machine in *Modern Times*, which I admit is funny.) The dog gives the audience a really helpless look each time this starts up again. It's the relentless nature of these labor-saving devices, their *non*-intuitive qualities, that confuses Hulot in the Arpels' kitchen.

The later cartoon is *Design for Leaving* of 1954, in which Daffy Duck installs a fantastic number of machines in Elmer Fudd's house, devices that threaten to destroy it. There's a fire-extinguishing robot, again with the little sphere for a head, but with a fireman's helmet on it, that rushes in and douses the slightest source of heat with a bucket of water, then zooms back into its sinister closet.

But Tati is always kindly. Sure there's a European gloom, maybe even a Buddhist gloom at the heart of his vision, but the films are basically affectionate about being alive, about our having to live together, with all this idiotic, dangerous junk we've made.

I've seen many prints of *Les Vacances de M. Hulot* in many places, dubbed, cut and mangled. I've sometimes had the feeling that I was watching a version that had been wrongly assembled. But the nature of *Hulot* is that it's a series of panel cartoons – not a comic strip and not a plot or scenario. It's like a glorious issue of the *New Yorker* from the Forties or Fifties come alive. Richard Lester commented on Tati's camera – 'You have all hell breaking loose in the frame.'

The early shot of the lobby of the Hôtel de la Plage could be a masterful *ligne claire* tableau by Hergé or Joost Swarte, or in Gluyas Williams's india ink. From above we see all the guests in their coteries or grumpy individual pursuits. We know them immediately.

In terms of hotels, dining rooms, waiters and so on, there's a common humor *Les Vacances* shares with Ludwig Bemelmans – the Hôtel de la Plage could easily be the hotel on the Ile d'Yeu in *The Best of Times*. Bemelmans was someone who also gently reminded us Americans that Europe was there, had always been there and should be part of us, not only with *Madeline* but in *Hotel Splendide*, set in New York but in a wholly European-run grand hotel.

About 1987 I went to see a pretty good print of *Les Vacances de M. Hulot* with my friend Seán Bradley. It was in Edinburgh, on an inviting autumn Sunday evening. Seemed perfect. Here's what the citizens of Edinburgh did not laugh at that night:

Men, women and children rushing from one railway platform to another as the announcer on the public address system constantly reorders the tracks for holiday trains. The two tangled *parapluies*. The sounds of Hulot's car. The wind blowing through the hotel lobby; the riddle of the black footprints leading up the stairs. The groaning borborygmus of the door to the dining room. They didn't laugh at Hulot's killer tennis playing, with its mysterious frying-pan move, or stir a cheek muscle at the car tyre funeral wreath that deflates, or the feather in the hat of the old lady moving along the receiving-line which tickles everyone in the face. Nor could they bring themselves to laugh at

Hulot trapped in his folding boat, which starts to look like a shark. They wouldn't laugh at his stepping on the tow rope and being twanged into the canal. They would not even laugh at the bolus of salt water taffy slowly seeping off a hook on the confectioner's cart, which disturbs Hulot so much he constantly starts to lurchingly run at it, in order to save it, and they *certainly* were not going to laugh at the vicious-looking little fox rug that gets stuck on the spur of Hulot's riding boot while he's waiting for the pretty girl and nearly frightens him to death when he leans down to tap out his pipe.

We almost suffocated from laughing at Tati but also at this weird, but typically Edinburgh, audience. Going to a Jacques Tati movie – what a moment to repress yourselves! When the lights came up I had decided to leave the country.

– Horror Feebs of the Fifties! –

T he banalities of horror. After you've read Beckett you know that life is bad enough without having to watch a giant bloodshot eye with teeth chewing up art deco skyscrapers.

Horror is about male self-hatred. It's the same impulse that drives 'disaster' movies. Men look at the world they've created (nuclear weapons, McDonalds, special bass fishing boats) and it disgusts them. Their only answer is to see what it would be like to destroy it all. These are the acts of hypocrites and onanists.

I had a friend named Joe Bellini. It was with him that I went to the only two horror movies that I ever paid to see – it was a Christopher Lee double bill, *Dracula* and *Dracula, Prince of Darkness*, so it must have been in 1966. I was thirteen. These aren't particularly frightening movies. They have more to do with costumes than anything else. And maybe tits. Blood sucking was surprisingly far down the list.

I remember only three things about this: 1) My mom didn't want me to go. 2) Christopher Lee's fangs looked very professional. 3) It was sort of cool when he turned into dust.

Bellini was severely interested in horror. He introduced me to Lon Chaney, built his own guillotine (I think by now he's built many) and became a professional makeup artist and a sculptor for various wax museums. In more recent years he has produced a series of ghoulish collectable dolls – one of them a figure of Charlotte Corday.

He once constructed a big wound on my face out of latex, collodion and Technicolor blood that made my mother plotz. He was very keen to develop some super suave fangs like Christopher Lee's, and he went so far as to consult with a dental laboratory about it.

He owned an 8mm print of the complete Chaney *Phantom of the Opera*, and once made a tape recorded sound track for it, which I was invited to view. Despite his love for Lon Chaney, it was rather satiric: after Mary Philbin beholds the Phantom's sleeping chamber, in Joe's version she stumbles through the next several scenes mumbling repeatedly, 'I saw a coffin . . . I saw a coffin.'

We also watched *Man of a Thousand Faces*, which is James Cagney in the life story of Lon Chaney. It's a terrible movie, but frankly there's stuff in it that's psychologically icky (though inept) and much more disturbing than anything in a real Lon Chaney picture. Giving a severe beating to an actual cripple is creepier than wearing a rubber head.

Everyone grew up with Godzilla, at school they were always talking about Godzilla, you couldn't get away from Godzilla, but I preferred Rodan. He was a big old pterodactyl. *Rodan* was often to be seen on TV Saturday afternoons; Fard and I got to know it very well. I thought it a much better picture than *Godzilla*, although it was the same old story: some kind of *Japanese bumbling* leads to the wholesale punishment of mankind by creating giant atomic mutants or freeing scads of long-dormant Mesozoic critters. Rodan himself brings to light some large caterpillars that live in a tunnel. Anyway the supersonic wind from Rodan's big wings knocks over the Asahi brewery. It's since been rebuilt.

Some people are just happy to watch HORROR no matter how bad it is. Is this as true for any other genre?

What about *The Manster*, where a guy is given an injection by an Evil Scientist (a profession that has died out, in the movies anyway). His shoulder gets really sore and the next thing he knows the sore is an EYE and pretty soon he's got a whole extra head. What about *Monster on the Campus* (guy in a monkey costume)? What about *Robot Monster* (guy in a monkey costume *and* a space helmet)? What about *Them!*, which is just a bunch of ants?

Consider *Attack of the Mushroom People*, a new low in rubber-head technology. I remember seeing some fungally-related American cheapie where there was only money enough for one complete warty costume, so the rest of the actors playing the mutants were given one body part each and a black leotard and told to try to hide behind trees, each menacingly waving a bulbous hand or leg. I remember very distinctly Fard turning to me in the half light (we drew the drapes for watching Saturday afternoon monster movies) and saying, 'This isn't scary.' We turned off the TV and opened the curtains and there was Southern California, which was much scarier.

Horror movies are like pop music – you need your own. No other countries can really bring them off. The Brits laboured mightily on *The Giant Behemoth* (as opposed to all those tiny little behemoths), but ye gods, it's just stiff upper lip all the way until the thing briefly, risibly, wades out of the sea and knocks a few things over.

Not to be outstripped by Ancient Egypt, Mexico tried to make an antihero out of Popoca, an *Aztec* mummy, but he wasn't even wrapped up right and he quickly ended up picking on girls. Forget it.

In college, Isidor and I were big fans of these pictures, especially *Wrestling Women vs. The Aztec Mummy*, but this was when we thought that Popoca's name was *Xochitl*, which made him much more interesting. It even sounded a little bit Yiddish.

I always liked mummies, and I suppose I allowed myself to be frightened by them; at least I tried to join in. As with all these things, the first, *The Mummy* with Boris Karloff, was the best. There is something a little scary about tombs and braziers and sarcophagi, but this is nearly always ruined by dialogue like *And do you know, Englishman, why he has come back to life? For three thousand years he has vowed vengeance upon the descendants of the desecrators of his tomb – the murderers of his young bride, blablabla.* And there's not a lot of action.

There was a witty man named Bob Wilkins who was a 'horror movie host' – another vanished profession – on television in San Francisco. He didn't dress up in capes or anything. Instead he wore rather beautifully tailored suits and languorously smoked a cigar as he commented laconically on the evening's offerings, many of which were very, very bad. The humorist Jeff Shaffer and I went to interview him in the 70s and we were talking about mummy movies and Wilkins said, 'Personally I've never understood why mummies are supposed to be frightening. They're very slow-moving – you can push them right over. Also, they're fire traps.' He was right. The fastest-moving thing in *The Mummy's Hand* is George Zucco's Adam's apple.

No one is scared by what horror movie makers try to scare you with. But I'll tell you what *is* scary. The way Jeff Goldblum walks when he's mostly fly. The thick swirl of birds up near the ceiling in *The Birds*. Not the man-frog in William Cameron Menzies's *The Maze*, but the shadow of an ornately carved armchair. The thin-lipped speckled face of *The Man From Planet X*.

In *The Tingler*, Vincent Price discovers that at moments of extreme terror an actual creature grows on your spine, something like a big crawdaddy. Naturally he'd like one of these, as he's no longer a lawyer, so he scares a lady to death in order to extract her tingler. What's alarming is not the murder or the tingler, but that Vincent Price has at the ready a *custom-made tingler carrying case*, just the right size, to put it in.

But none of these things was as scary as the undulating ribbon of light thrown on my bedroom wall every night by a gap in the window shade, or the *frazzled length of wire* coming out of the ceiling of the guest bedroom in my grandmother's house. Who needs horror movies since Covid and Bojo and Trump? Reality has outstripped the imaginations of the horror feebs. You don't have to watch *The Corpse Grinders*. Just switch on the news.

– *Casablanca* –

I s there anything worse than being a nineteen-year-old romantic? I sincerely doubt it and I sincerely pity me. In the middle ages one viewed romance as a help in life. Courtly love ensured that at least some parts of society ran smoothly. But that was before the movies, television, and Hugh Hefner. It probably wouldn't work now, but maybe we should try it.

Got romance from books of course but *Casablanca* didn't help. Being romantic took me to Manhattan, then brought me to Scotland, then back to America, and then Scotland. Scotland still isn't really as romantic to me as New York. I've been doing this my whole life and it's crazy. The amount of jet fuel alone is embarrassing, never mind what I was actually doing with my existence.

Yes, I am a self-wrecker.

Being a romantic made me follow V. down the stairs at the office because I thought her pink Converse hi-tops meant we were to be together. It once made me get very out of control on the Staten Island Ferry, saying the dumbest things I've ever heard to a girl I barely knew – then to invade her apartment and get too sozzled on Cointreau to leave.

Romance insists I suspend a tassel from the scroll of my very unremarkable violin, which I can't play for beans. It's a hindrance, not a help, take it from me. It does mean that I am willing to listen to the romantic stories of others, but actually I don't know any other romantics. Everyone I know seems more like an elevator, or a calculator.

But I had this girlfriend and I was going to try to impress her. I, this cesspool of callowness and sperm from California. She was from New Jersey. Her father was a printer, a profession I always held in respect; he wore turtlenecks and liked *Tosca* and things like that.

One of the few advantages I had in intellectual parley with my girl was my movie chops. I found out she'd never seen *Casablanca* and I rubbed it in. Just enough. So here we were on upper Broadway on a warm night. I was wearing the absurd antiromantic wine-coloured double-knit trousers that followed me through college. I couldn't get rid of them.

She didn't know much about movies and since I had grown up with very little else in my head I thought that this, *this* was where I would strike.

We had fooled around pretty heavily in the Museum of Modern Art's screening room, during *On the Avenue* with Dick Powell. In *Casablanca* we didn't fool around – I wanted her to see it, after all, because it's romantic. It's also horny as hell, though – what I call the Bottle Scene, when Ingrid comes back after the cafe is closed. It's dominated by a big bottle of bourbon in the foreground, bigger than everyone, and Humphrey drinks most of it. How brimming everything is.

Believe it or not, in the late Sixties and early Seventies cinema-going was just re-emerging as a cool or even acceptable thing to do (to take an interest in it, as opposed to merely going to the movies). Woody Allen did a lot to promote the idea of film as a necessary and usual part of life – he showed people standing in line at the New Yorker cinema, *in a movie*, which was inspiring.

But going to the movies in New York felt weird, after suburbia. They sell the same Mason Dots and all that, but you never feel quite as protected, or diverted, in a New York cinema as you do in the Fox Fullerton. The streets are too close. And New Yorkers are more matter-of-fact about going to the pictures. It's just one item on their vast list of daily rights.

The exception, of course, is Radio City Music Hall, which envelops, cradles, hypnotizes and suckles you so completely it's like being in a wonderful expensive coffin of velvet and black marble and gold. It's like being Lenin in his mausoleum, only with the Rockettes.

I've spent some of the most important days of my life in the West Eighties and Nineties. You wouldn't call it one of the romantic neighbourhoods of Manhattan, but a lot happened to me there. The Thalia cinema was on West 95th – it's gone now, or rather it's been absorbed by a general arts centre next door. It smelled a little funny to a Californian nose. I don't think my girl had been to the Thalia before that night.

I can tell you the truth: I didn't know much about *Casablanca* either. We knew it was cool, though – there were just as many Humphrey Bogart posters in the dormitories as there were of that photograph of the Marx Brothers with a hookah, or reproductions of Toulouse-Lautrecs and Van Goghs and Rousseaus. Lots of things were being rediscovered as cool, as opposed to now, where it seems that just everything is cool, no question. Even downtown Milwaukee, Wisconsin. They insist on its *retro coolness*.

When you're young *Casablanca* strikes you as a romance with some solid Hollywood politics thrown in. But you could say it's propaganda, or even a war movie with Ingrid Bergman floating on top. It's a movie that looks like it's going to lose itself, then comes back strong in the last reel, and there aren't many pictures that pull that off. Once a movie has set itself adrift, it usually disappears over the horizon.

Casablanca doesn't contain the whole world. *Au Hasard Balthazar* it isn't, but it has tragedy, comedy, love and death enough for a summer evening.

There are many things to like about *Casablanca*; not the stuff that everybody likes, but secret, sweet things. One, perhaps, is that the writers were making it up as they went along. That's sort of how we felt about everything in the Seventies anyway. There's the big dark clayey globe in the beginning, the narrator of the prologue who says 'Wiwld waw,' the animated bumps of the embarkation points on the map.

There's the little brandy glass Carl has in his pocket. The textiles dealer holding the price card in his hand, at the corner of the lace he's trying to sell to Ingrid. The range of official fezzes. Water pipes and Turkish coffee pots. Sydney Greenstreet's fly-swatter: there's punctuation and symbolism in that. The way he uses it and when. The look of the documents. The caviar in its special bowl of ice, the odd telephone in the hangar – a phone with a roof – almost as weird as the miniature Eiffel Tower that holds glassware in the 'Belle Aurore'.

Peter Lorre, in macassar oil and a dinner jacket that fits, nimble with his drinks and cigarettes, delivering some of the best lines ever written. *You despise me, don't you?* The way Lorre and S. Z. Sakall and Paul Henreid talk – the way they all talk! Ingrid Bergman's delivery. The *diction*, the almost unfair, sinister vocal clarity of the thing.

The small, winsome lights embedded in the concrete of the runway, in the last scene. It's amazing that little winsome lights on the ground in fog didn't become the norm for scenes of brave romantic sacrifice.

The resemblance of the interiors of Rick's Café Américain and Lundy Brothers' fish restaurant in Sheepshead Bay, Brooklyn. Arches. Adobe, or whatever they call it in Morocco. Moorish plastering. Big rooms with oriental chandeliers giving off dappled light, imbuing the finnan haddie at $3.35 with real nuance. At least a year before I discovered that I actually liked to eat fish, and could barely gag it down, I'd get on the B train anytime in order to eat lunch in that surrogate Rick's.

TOTAL 'MARSEILLAISE' THROAT LUMP

There's no denying that this occurs – it's medically recognized. People often present themselves at emergency rooms watery-eyed and unable to speak after a showing of *Casablanca*. Doctors know this is due not to the 'We'll always have Paris' stuff, but to the moment when the Nazis are singing *Watch on the Rhine* and Paul Henreid steps up to the band and orders them to play the 'Marseillaise'. Max Steiner engineered this intuitive, Charles Ivesian meld of the two anthems.

There are many achievements of France – wines from the Loire, Braille, roux, Renoir and diacritical marks all come to mind – but perhaps the incontestable French accomplishment is that everyone in every country in the world gets a lump in the throat and starts to blub when they hear the 'Marseillaise'. *Casablanca* may have something to do with that, but it wouldn't have been in the movie if its makers didn't already know that it was like suddenly slicing a Bermuda onion right on your face.

One feels doubly stirred − it's important to save Warner Brothers *and* France.

My great-great uncle Zephyr died of 'Marseillaise' Throat Lump at a France-America Friendship Day in Omaha, Nebraska in 1926. He was of French extraction, but several others also succumbed.

That many national anthems are total crap helps. You could say that the 'Marseillaise' was one of the great secret weapons of the war. It was stored in a bomb proof vault in Hollywood, and they knew just when to use it.

Last year I went through a phase of listening to the 'Internationale' while struggling to wake up in the morning and make breakfast. I thought it would buck me up, and it's not bad. But I came back to the 'Marseillaise'. You can squeeze grapefruit to it. Even if you won't be able to swallow your egg.

I wish I still smoked. However, there's nothing *to* smoke. Rick and Louis and Ugarte and Victor all got to smoke Camels, Gauloises and Dimitrinos from the look of things. *Casablanca* is a whirlpool of tobacco smoke, champagne, bourbon and cognac. The eroticism of its smoke drifts through almost every shot.

2 Décembre 1941. That's the date on the chit we see Rick sign when we finally get in to the cafe. On the table is an empty champagne saucer − his hand taps a bishop − he's playing chess with himself and smoking − then we see him.

Bogart drinks and smokes more than everyone else in *Casablanca*. He smokes for us all. During the picture he smokes about twenty-one cigarettes – that last one is quite something and I'll get back to it. (You don't always see the cigarettes being lit, so I'm going roughly by length.) The continuity people were pretty good and that must have meant that Humphrey got to light up more than necessary. He'd have liked that.

Peter Lorre, surprisingly, smokes only three or four cigarettes, but he's not around very long. He's smoking almost the whole time he's on camera. Very few actors ever got as much out of a cigarette.

The other cigarette pro is Paul Henreid. He should have copyrighted that double whammy he used to enchant Bette Davis in *Now, Voyager*. Instead he selflessly offered it to all mankind. In *Casablanca* he smokes ten to Bogart's twenty. You keep expecting him to 'Bette' his cigarettes with Ilsa but he restrains himself; anyway Ilsa doesn't smoke so it would have been pretty funny if he kept doing that. He smokes alone, so that we see his beautiful hands.

Claude Rains smokes seven cigarettes on screen. He's a casually elegant smoker, of course. He smokes in easy moments, to be dapper, rather than when things are tough. Sam is seen to have a couple of cigarettes smouldering in an ashtray on top of his piano; Carl smokes a cigarette after business hours, when he's doing the accounts. Sydney Greenstreet smokes a cigar, in the Blue Parrot, with an air that suggests it's usual with him. He doesn't have to be elegant.

Conrad Veidt rarely has a cigarette, but when he does he smokes it right down to the end of civilization.

Through the smoke you can just see the plot shimmer like a mirage in fumes of alcohol. This too is pleasant, though you wonder if in 1941 there really was that much western liquor in Morocco. Of course booze goes where it's needed. Everybody in Rick's is engaged in Moorish plastering. Rick has nine or ten drinks. One of them is pretty much a whole bottle of bourbon. He's upset. Predictably, Victor Laszlo is in second place, as you would expect of the unelected leader of the free world, with six drinks and an iced coffee. (When Victor and Ilsa first come into Rick's, they sit down and Victor asks for two Cointreaus, the same stunt he pulls on Bette in *Now, Voyager*! Does he always push Cointreau on women?)

Ilsa matches him pretty closely with five drinks, although she is rarely seen to drink them. She's so pure. We get it. (She likes that iced coffee of Sydney's, though – she says she will miss it *in America*. Is this some kind of snide screenwriters' impugning of coffee in America, maybe specifically coffee in Los Angeles? I hope so.) Claude Rains has five drinks, but as with his smoking it's more a matter of style and gesture. Louis likes women, not drink. Before he's arrested Peter Lorre probably has three or four drinks, Sam has maybe two, and Carl has a small brandy with the elderly German couple.

It's Glassware vs. Nazis

Everybody drinks, and because it's Warner Brothers there's glassware to match. Cognac glasses, champagne saucers, little brandy ponies (like the one in Carl's pocket), some ugly cut glass shot glasses in Rick's office, an important brandy glass that Rick sets upright after the disturbance of Ugarte's arrest. The 'two Cointreaus' come in amazingly small little conical glasses, while the Champagne cocktails arrive in schooners, it seems. There are even American shot glasses, for bourbon, at the Blue Parrot!

There are two points awash in only Champagne: the flashback to Rick and Ilsa's affair in Paris, and any table where the Nazis gather. Louis, the swine, has recommended Veuve Cliquot. Yvonne's rogue Nazi is drinking Champagne too. The Nazis know they've destroyed Europe and they're drinking up what's left of it fast.

But glassware becomes unimportant as the four main characters are drawn back into the global struggle. Perhaps the only drink casually tossed back is a shot of something in a highball glass Rick gives Victor after he's escaped from the raid (behind them is a colossal *fortification* of assorted barware: alcohol has been a bulwark against the Germans). In fact that's the last glass of *anything* in *Casablanca*, except for the grubby tumbler of Vichy water which Louis decides not to drink.

Counting the drinks says more about Hollywood than it does about French Morocco, or even World War II. Drinking and smoking added a lot to atmosphere in movies. Alcohol makes things look as if everyone's rich and/or desperate; smoking gave actors a whole repertoire of gesture and nuance they hadn't had before, and that photographed strikingly. And they don't have these opportunities now.

Paul Henreid, Bette Davis, Humphrey Bogart or Peter Lorre smoking anything.

The first part of *Casablanca* is a descent into hell, the confused and corrupt situation the refugees are in, mirrored in the social strata and the layers of smoke in Rick's. Everyone's given up. The tobacco smoke and the booze help to obscure the light of reality. Humphrey's the most bummed-out of the bunch and he's socking everything away, surrounding himself with a toxic vapour because that's what it feels like in his head. But then when he's slapped awake, as it were, by Ilsa's arrival in Casablanca, and he decides to do something about her, he begins to emerge from his poisonous cloud. He sobers. He refuses Sydney's bourbon at the Blue Parrot – he even drinks *coffee* (the drink Ilsa prefers). When we find him studying the letters of transit, he isn't even smoking! He doesn't smoke again until Victor and Ilsa are on the plane. Then he allows himself a luxurious 'post-coital' cigarette; he's just had an underground political orgasm.

He doesn't offer one to Louis. Louis is too cynical. It's not 'black and white', unless you watch it on television. In real life, *Casablanca* and so many of those Warner Brothers dramas are a shifting, seductive spectrum of smooth, deep blacks, ivories and crème de cafes. The intense sunlight (Californian, of course, but say it's like Morocco) is the glare of the harsh world, the world of war everyone's trying to shun. The life desired takes place indoors, mainly at night, when these beleaguered people can say what it is that they want.

The sun is filtered through venetian blinds and jalousies, making patterns of bars and stripes fall on the action. Everyone's in jail. This isn't a motif pushed to its *perfect yet infernal limit* as Douglas Sirk used to do. In Sirk pictures there are so many physical symbols, so many things in the way, so many flowers and decorative screens and menacing vases, that by the end of the movie the actors have to pick their way around the sets and the script like they're in a junk shop.

What the stripes say (they're also on Ilsa's blouse, and the cage-like grid of bamboo poles above her at the market) is that nothing is black and white. Stripes are actually a gray area of existence, not this or that for long. Like the desires of those in Rick's, in Casablanca itself, like the meaning of Vichy. And when the fog of confusion and dishonesty and war envelops the airport and the murder of Strasser, and Victor and Ilsa fly into the future, Rick and Louis are clearing their heads. Now they know what to do. And that's romantic.

I didn't think my girlfriend was enjoying it much, though she laughed at the line about not invading certain parts of New York – everybody did. It's one of the reasons you go to see *Casablanca* in New York. I wanted her to like it, though, because then we'd have something to share.

Once she clicked her tongue and said she thought something corny. It probably was, though now it drives me crazy – what could it have been? Rick helping the Bulgarian couple? What??

All was not well there in the Thalia that evening. Granted this was 1972 and *Casablanca* was just coming back into its own, but this was the worst print of anything I'd ever seen. One in four lines of dialogue was missing or made absurd by evisceration – often there would be that ominous fluttering sound after a splice goes through the gate and lifts the film off the sound drum, so the next few words sound like someone has slammed a door on you in the middle of an argument. There were blisters, bits from other prints cut in – it got worse and worse and *worse*. We weren't exactly enjoying the visual luxuriance I described earlier. It was like reading a good book from a library that's covered in old fashioned Scotch tape, coffee stains, foxing and with some of the corners torn off. Yes, it's all there, but it messes with your head while you're trying to love it.

I once had a used copy of the Norton *Modern Poems* edited by Ellmann and O'Clair. On the page where I was *trying* to read Wallace Stevens's *Anecdote of the Jar*, two students in a classroom had been writing notes to each other in the margin:

> *My pussy sheds.*
> *Not my problem!!!*

Is what I'm talking about.

So in the Thalia that night there was brooding, serious unrest about the quality of the print. A jungle drums level of trouble. Most of the people in the Thalia seemed to be guys in their mid twenties with tinted glasses and beards – film buffs – a few had girlfriends in loose dresses. They all looked stoned and at one moment I wondered if this was what happened to you if you *went to the movies too much.*

Isn't this the rarest type of discomfiture? Trying to enjoy something you like, with someone you like or maybe even love, and it's not working out? Even though it's dark, you see them looking skeptical.

But now came the *coup de grâce*, and the reason I hardly ever went back to the Thalia and didn't weep at its demise along with the *New York Times*, for this is how this print of *Casablanca* ended:

RENAULT: *Major Strasser has been shot. Round up the usual suspects.*
CUT TO 'MARSEILLAISE'. END TITLE.
GIRLFRIEND: *Hey, what kind of an ending do you call that?*
ME: *But –*

No Hill of Beans, no Beautiful Friendship, no NOTHIN'. CUT BACK TO THALIA THEATER, INT. The film buffs were going nuts, yelling, screaming, tearing their hair out. Some of them were standing on the seats, shaking their fists at the projection room, the girlfriends clawing at their combat jackets. Mason Dots were being thrown. The house lights were coming up very slowly, as if the little cinema was itself waking to disaster or war. Ask for your money back? How would that compensate you for *Casablanca* being forever herniated?

We left the buffs to their war and bald spots and went out onto Broadway. It was hot and we walked past the supermarket where in *The Odd Couple* Walter Matthau whacks chocolate ice cream all over Jack Lemmon's Brooks Brothers 'Tropical Weight' suit.

I was looking for little winsome lights on the ground – it wasn't going to work out. I didn't know it then, but I was terribly much not what these people wanted for their daughter. Later on there was a terrible argument at the George Washington Bridge. There was an I Can't Marry You moment in a Volkswagen beetle (hers, and yes, hers). She got rid of me and I don't blame her. I noticed I was going around in Bogartian deeps. It's the question about Scotland and Calvinism – which needed the other more? Was I bitter in my love life *before* I encountered Humphrey Bogart, or did he school me in it?

Rick overcame all this male pain – he found a way to live with it. Someone hurts you like this, you drink and smoke. You learn to play chess by yourself. I began to see my girlfriend's father as my Victor Laszlo. I did lose out. But we'd always have Englewood Cliffs.

It's not wanting to be *tough* like Humphrey Bogart, it's wanting to be *sad* like Humphrey Bogart.

– *Chinatown* –

Wet Books in Los Angeles

One of the reasons I write this is to remind myself that just as in poems and novels there are wild, evocative pleasures we take in movies that are *ours* – they're not forced on us by the writer or the director because they can't be, or at least they couldn't have been submitted and approved. Things about a movie you like that would really perplex or enrage its makers, if you told them. Private, covetous things. How about the really enjoyable sequence of the bookstores in *The Big Sleep*? It's in the first part of the movie, the part with the brains and the wit. The Chandler part. The second half is a sour, frenzied reference to Bogartism, without chemistry, and makes almost no sense – fingerprints of the censors.

The Big Sleep was shot almost completely on sound stages, and you can tell, but in its artificial rain there's something convincing, a kind of romantic rainy world it's easy to accept – possibly because Los Angeles in the rain seems so unreal anyway. Chandler was adept at discovering small aspects of romance in L.A. This is something he passed on to us.

Humphrey Bogart's on the trail of a blackmailer

pornographer pervert esthete, who fronts his activities with an antiquarian bookshop. Humphrey studies up quick on modern first editions in the *Hollywood Public Library* – we're shown this explicitly. The blonde library lady flirts with him (in fact every woman in this movie, lead and bit, flirts with him). Then he goes to the evil esthete's shop and pretends to be a goofy bookworm, and discovers that the blackmailing pervert's secretary doesn't really know anything about rare books. So: RACKET. I really like the way this bookshop is depicted. Do you like the look of Kim Novak's African art shop in *Bell, Book and Candle*? Me too. The *Big Sleep* bookshop has fancy lettering in the window, a few fey *objets d'art* around, and not too many books – exactly the way rare bookshops used to look. When there were some. Humphrey retreats across the street to the 'Acme' book shop, a much less rarified place, with lots of books in it for one thing, where the Babe in Glasses lets her hair down and tells him everything he needs to know about the antiquarian pervert. There's a dissolve – they've spent some time together! You've been in bookshops on rainy days – is there anything nicer? It's certainly better than sitting in some stinky movie theater – O there's no comparison and you know it.

There's a rare bookshop scene in *Vertigo* with almost the same purpose and fond affect. (Does the Strand masquerade as Pageant in *Hannah and Her Sisters*?) There's the brave Polish wartime bookshop in *To Be or Not To Be*, and another really classy one in *The Last Mitterrand* (not a front this time).

William Faulkner, Jules Furthman and Leigh Brackett, who wrote *The Big Sleep*, liked this milieu, you can tell. They probably hung around the good bookshops of L.A. quite a bit – they might have been the *reason* there were good out of print shops in L.A., and still are. Chandler would have liked them too. Except for Leigh Brackett they were all from somewhere else, and so were the books. They probably really liked it when it rained.

It Begins for Us

One day in 1974 I was finishing a broadcast – we worked at this radio station – and on the other side of the glass I saw Isidor burst into the control room, panting. He was clearly waiting for me to get off the air. Very jumpy. I closed the show and went down the hall. What's with you? I said. *You gotta see this movie*, he said. *It's unbelievable. Get your coat.*

So we went to some theater, it's funny I can't remember which. It might have been the Trans-Lux. It was still afternoon and the place was packed. So what is this, I said, what's it all about? Isidor sat staring straight ahead in his seat. *You'll see.*

From the Thirties style of the opening credits of *Chinatown*, you can tell this is going to be a uniquely meticulous movie. What had no doubt riveted Isidor was the intricacy of the thought involved, and the elegance of the dialogue, not to mention the performances. This was the day on which Isidor abandoned as his heroes B. B. King and whoever wrote *Beowulf* and replaced them with Jack Nicholson. For me the compelling nature of *Chinatown* was the picture it gave of Southern California, whence I had been cruelly wrenched at the age of eleven – even though I knew that if our family had remained there I would have become a surfer and compulsive masturbator and never would have got to New York. I retain a childhood love of adobe style houses, orange groves, crickets at about eight p.m., blue sky, sunsets and so on. For I had once had a sensual Californian existence: I never wore a coat and on a summer day I could put one black olive at the end of each finger and eat them one by one. Much as I liked New York I was always a little homesick for California; so on a gut, locale and morale level this movie really got to me and may have been the reason that I somewhat later decided to leave New York and go back to California, leaving Isidor, Paddy's Clam House and a redhead all behind, how dumb.

There in the Trans-Lux, if it was the Trans-Lux, I was regressing, wallowing in an esthetic I thought I had lost forever, while Isidor, a committed New Yorker, was *turning into* Jack Nicholson. I was so arrested by the visuals that I don't think I took in the drama at that first viewing. I peppered Isidor with questions about the plot as we were walking back across town.

Some of it is a little confusing, of course, and some of these problems become more complex the more you watch the picture, rather than less. I doubt that anyone who only watched *Chinatown* once or twice would have puzzled at these things as have Isidor and I. We stopped at Park Avenue and 59th Street and Isidor, who was finding my questions infuriating, spoke in the voice of Jack: *Let me tell you something, pal. The only way you're going to figure any of this out is by going back in there.* So we turned around and walked east to the next showing.

It Gets a Hold of Us

Over the following weeks and months we went to see *Chinatown* absolutely as often as we could, that is, as often as we could afford it. We got so hipped on it that we started going separately, competing on the number of times we'd seen it, rather than enjoying it together. It wasn't exactly acrimonious but it got a little tense. Isidor told me he'd seen it three times one Sunday and I couldn't bear to talk to him again until I'd caught up. His girlfriend broke up with him because of all the Jack Nicholson impressions and compulsive *Chinatown* matinées.

The more we saw it the more it 'meant', and I say this advisedly. We were in a kind of mania about it, where an increasing amount of dialogue from the picture seemed not only to apply to, but to *solve*, almost everything in our lives. Shakespeare didn't have a patch on it. I can't believe how many times in the 1970s I answered a perfectly civil question, from anybody, with 'Let me tell you something, pal . . . '

Isidor was more threatening in his delivery. A waitress in a coffee shop asked us if we wanted water, and Isidor, switching to Lou Escobar mode, roared at her, *WATER!?* and glowered at her so, that someone else was deputized to bring us our hamburgers. It was as if it was his personal mission to make everything in the movie mean everything to everybody in the world.

This didn't help with dating.

We were hooked on this thing. We even started wearing our neckties tucked into our shirts about two buttons down, like John Huston. When someone asked us why we were doing that, either Isidor gave them the sharp side of Jake Gittes's tongue or we didn't answer them. Would Noah Cross explain himself?

Now we're getting old, this goddamn movie still has far too much significance for us. It's still how we communicate. It's NUTS. Isidor is a professor – he has a *job*. How has he managed to hold onto it all these years, given that when anyone asks him what he's doing, out comes *As little as possible*?

The Beauties of Chinatown

To someone who is uneasy not to be in California (my wife catches me staring balefully at the thermometer in Scotland), *Chinatown* is a beautiful and poignant movie. Its *climatic* (not dramatic) atmosphere is riveting to me. This is quite an achievement, as there's hardly a breath in it of modern Los Angeles, or of the 1970s (a poor decade which looked poor on film). This obtains right down to the lighting, even the ambient noise. For an L.A. kid of the Fifties and Sixties, that's exciting in itself, the immersion in the past that Polanski, Richard Sylbert and John Alonzo accomplished. *Chinatown* was one of the first Hollywood pictures, if not *the* first, to take the past seriously in terms of design; previously there had always been a nod to contemporary styling (so that the hoi polloi would actually *go to the picture*, and not faint at Deborah Kerr's coiffure). Look at the depiction of the 1920s in *Singin' in the Rain* or the deportment in *Drums Along the Mohawk*, Julie Christie's style in *Doctor Zhivago*, the big shouldered dresses in the 1940 *Pride and Prejudice* that turn Jane Austen's characters into Munchkins. Or just anything. They didn't really give a damn, despite all their 'research'. Before 1974 and this movie, *Chinatown*, whether the actors were wearing top hats or bonnets, everyone looked like they were in a *Look* magazine Christmas ad for Coca-Cola.

John Alonzo managed to photograph various kinds of *heat* in a surprising way in *Chinatown*, capturing even the memory of heat, in the valley, at evening, or the anticipation of a hot day, as Gittes drives up towards the Mulwrays' home: an evocation of a summer morning in a pristine old Southern California neighborhood: the promising blue sky behind the gracious Spanish-style mansion, its mixture of shrubs and trees, the fountain. There's the same sort of moment at the old folks' home at the end of the day when Gittes has been shot at in the (perfectly colored) orange grove – the hints of western purple in the twilight behind this building (also Spanish-style) and the contrast with the neon sign: 'Mar Vista Rest Home', a name straight out of Chandler.

Gittes at Evelyn's home after he's been beaten and shot at: the night, the crickets, the lighting, the sound of the fountain: an audible reminder of water which recurs and soothes and torments. The bathroom.

The bridge, the binoculars, the hats. Hats! Whenever Gittes, Escobar and Loach are in the frame together, it's a battle of hats.

Echo Park: the muted greenery, the soft focus of the heat haze, all in a satin-textured picture postcard from the 1930s. And in the *expanses* of this movie, the hills, the beach, the sea, the vast fruit groves, the dry river beds (evocative of an earlier epic of water and California, King Vidor's *Our Daily Bread*), you see very clearly what California used to be – what it had to offer. Why it captured the imagination of people all over America, many of them numbskulls and crooks. In *Chinatown* the riches of the place are its downfall. 'Chinatown' becomes a code word for a floating world of entrenched, unshakable corruption; Robert Towne got a lot from Frank Norris and Upton Sinclair. And to find menace in this beauty, *Chinatown* owes something to John Ford's *The Grapes of Wrath*, where the riches of California can never be enjoyed.

The mesmerizing shot of Mulwray standing on the beach, looking up at the culvert which has gushed 'dirty' water like an ejaculation – it's a moment of crisis for him. Suddenly the lighthouse flares out behind him, like an idea – he knows he's in deep shit.

A more subtly arresting scene is Gittes's lunch with Noah Cross on the island of Catalina: the understated beauty of the millionaire's hat, braces, his *ranchero's* shirt, the beautiful charbroiled fish served with its beady eye, the thrilling color of those two glasses of chilled Chardonnay. The servant; his jacket. *Just . . . find the girl.* It's like something out of the French court; gold and whispers.

Ida, the murdered chippy, sprawled on her kitchen floor among pitiful groceries, is straight out of religious art, or police photographs; when Gittes finally gets home after that busy day getting punched, shot at, having his wound reopened, making love with Mrs. Mulwray and then having to chase her all over the map, there's a still moment, almost a holy painting of him, as he pauses after a shower in his absurd pajamas, his head bowed, before turning off the light.

All day there has been a struggle between water and power.

The two problems of the movie are water and daughter.

Chinatown is a great tragedy because it contains some very good jokes. Aside from the horror of the moment, the slicing of Gittes's nose causes him to look comic in several subsequent scenes, precisely when things are getting fatally unfunny and out of control. Gittes's very first contact with Mrs. Mulwray comes as he's telling a rather funny 1930s joke of the 'Tijuana bible' variety. Towne has fun with names – the barber's name is Barney and the mortician is Morty. At the opening, when the fake Mrs. Mulwray is telling Gittes she wants to hire him, his theatrical reluctance is amusing. There's even something blackly comic about Gittes's fight with the Okies in the orange grove – there's a comic-strip side to the violence in *Chinatown*, a use of the irony Chandler gave to Philip Marlowe, which helps indicate Gittes's attitude to Los Angeles and his job. He goes at it with the cheery, depressed determination of 'Offissa Pupp' in *Krazy Kat*.

Chinatown is a tribute to Hollywood, in a strange way, and to the place itself – *that land*, where all these people had to live. They had to live as if they were in a real place, not just in a movie. But movies are the only way to describe the place.

The Nose Shot

One must talk about the horror and surgical precision of the nostril-slitting scene (one of the film's treatments of sensationalism, also a nod to the Thirties), not to overlook its *cinematic* precision. The first time you see it, it scares hell out of you and makes you feel sick. The second time it's still craven and vile and you mutter things about Polanski under your breath. He's appeared only to inflict this wound. In subsequent viewings you know it's there, and how to handle it: you're an inveterate roller-coaster rider bracing your legs . . . Then you start to take an interest in the reactions of those around you. There was never a sound made like this in movie history. I boldly venture it: that the noise people make when Roman Polanski cuts Jack Nicholson's nose open was never made before 1974, and is only ever heard at showings of this picture. A tremulous, revolted, *betrayed* inward hiss; gas escaping from someone who's being given a good shaking.

When *Jaws* came out, I went to see it in a large, steeply raked suburban cinema. It was so steep that it took about half an hour to climb up to my seat; the head of the guy in front of me was at the level of my feet. And I was so far from the screen, way down below, that when the scary stuff started happening, there was time to witness hundreds of rows of people reeling backwards in their seats, screaming and covering their eyes or waving their arms, *my god why did we come in here, why? A shark is eating people*, row upon row, in succession. There was time for the guy next to me to say, 'Hey, look *out*, now . . .' I'll bet Spielberg never figured on that. I was so far removed from any real experience of the movie – I must have been at least a quarter of a mile away – that this troubling human tidal wave of paid-for fear *was* my experience of *Jaws*. And that is a great thing that happens in a movie theater sometimes – the audience is the show. There's a superb scene by Chester Himes where everyone's screaming in a horror movie and he's bugged by the lady behind him – she's screaming *too* much – but then he realizes she's screaming because the man next to her is dead.

China Girl

Our friend Caserta was the real movie maniac. He'd developed this 'system', if you want to call it that, for spending his days off at the movies. He'd get up early, buy a *New York Post* because it had the famous 'movie clock' in it, go to the Breakfast Club coffee shop on Broadway, and eat six doughnuts. Then he'd run out into the street, his *New York Post* under his arm, hail a cab, and speed to the first showing of the first movie of the day. This was New York in the Seventies, so they showed movies in the morning – there are lots of peo-ple in New York, get it? They go to the movies when-ever the hell they want.

As soon as the first picture ended, Caserta rushed

out of the theater, grabbed a taxi and was driven to wherever the next picture on his list was just starting. He could see six or seven first-run pictures in a day. There were rules: you had to stay in Manhattan, even if you could slot in a picture in Brooklyn (this saved money on taxi fares) but, more worryingly, the only food you were allowed to eat all day was movie food.

I did this with him a couple of times. It was exhilarating, but by the end of the day I started to mix things up – I confused scenes between *The Great Gatsby* and *Dirty Mary, Crazy Larry*, *That's Entertainment* and *Death Wish*. (I've never sorted them out – these pictures are a rat king in my head.) My digestion was destroyed by Jujyfruits and the whole thing cost about eight hundred dollars. Caserta liked *Chinatown* well enough, though he didn't dig it like we did. Isidor insisted that *Chinatown* could never be part of Movie Day and I'm glad.

Caserta continued to be a maniac. He and I went to a press screening of *Young Frankenstein* where there were cast members present; he believed Madeline Kahn was 'checking him out'. He even applied for a job at *Variety*, on the basis of *nothing*. Even though he told them about Movie Day, he was shouted out of the office, breaking his heel on the stairs and tumbling down into the street.

As a result, the world got another businessman. Actions have consequences, *Variety*.

As that year wore on, Isidor and I noticed that it was becoming harder to locate and see *Chinatown*. We couldn't understand this, and fell into a form of mourning. One rainy night we were sitting around, the usual, faintly hilarious unspoken idea, *there's nothing to do in this town*, between us. It's like we were in *Marty*. Isidor made a low noise and pushed the movie section of the *Daily News* at me. At the side of one page was a narrow column of ads for the adult movie theaters, one of which was showing *China Girl – Featuring Stars from the Movie Chinatown!* We hadn't seen *Chinatown* for several weeks. *We'd better look into this*, said Isidor. He looked at me glumly, then spoke as Gittes: *This kind of investigation can be hard on your pocketbook*. Well, if we had to go, we had to.

This grubby little cinema was way over on the East Side. I've never understood why they need pornography over there – they're all supposed to be happy. Braced with some Jack Daniel's, we sat through *China Girl*. It had, of course, a preposterous premise – some fat politician was going to be intercoursed to death by robotic hookers. But there he was, good old James Hong (Kahn, the Mulwrays' butler). He wasn't in the sex scenes, which were almost unendurable, but he played a menacing gangster disguised as a waiter. His big line was 'You forgot your check!' So we went around saying that, too.

It turned out that we'd been made bereft of *Chinatown* in those dark months, and had had to resort to *China Girl*, for a reason: Hollywood and money. Paramount had a little picture out that year called *The Godfather Part II*. It looked like it was going to sweep the Oscars, and it did. *Chinatown* won only for best screenplay, despite being nominated in every category under the sun. They'd sneakily pulled *Chinatown* out of the theaters and crammed them with *The Godfather Part II*, one of the worst movies ever made! Isidor could never tolerate Coppola's lack of technique, what he called 'those big fat fingers of his.' But of course they were right, because *Chinatown* only made thirty million dollars, most of it off me and Isidor, and *The Godfather Part II* made almost *two hundred million dollars*. But that kind of money *proves* it's no good!

Faye Dunaway

Everything is flawed. Living in the Seventies was very difficult. Whichever way you turned it was Faye Dunaway or Karen Black.

As I got to know *Chinatown* better, I developed a bitter distaste for Faye Dunaway's performance as Evelyn Mulwray. She seemed out of whack with what everyone else was doing, as if she'd decided in her dressing room that this was how 1930s women acted, and that was that. If we were in a bad mood, we used to mimic her delivery ('Yes you *can*, Mr. Gittes') and her way of stepping on the other actors' lines. We ganged up on her and perversely proclaimed her the one thing wrong with this otherwise perfect picture.

Now, FIFTY YEARS LATER, I appreciate Faye Dunaway. Her look and demeanor are appropriate, I begin to think, and my watching of the film no longer snags on her tricky moments. Evelyn Mulwray is a 'Chandler broad' – she didn't flinch at a parade of characters from the gutter being dragged through her life, and bad language amuses her. She is essentially Mrs. Grayle from *Farewell, My Lovely*, and Faye Dunaway got that right.

Isidor still comforts himself by remembering that the other actress they considered for Evelyn was Jane Fonda.

The Chandler Jaunt

I was working in an antiquarian book shop – so I told Isidor to come out and we'd go down to L.A. and investigate *Chinatown* stuff. He was broke after a summer of learning Latin all at once, but he came. On the *bus*. After three days of Greyhound he looked like Ratso Rizzo. Isidor had never been west. The first night he was there my mother served him an artichoke and he thought we were playing a trick on him.

I rented this Chevrolet with a tiny motor and we infuriated just about everyone on Highway 101 all the way to Hollywood. Izzy had taken to wearing a 1940s kind of male hat which with his shades gave him an unsavoury look. He hadn't shaved either. Some of the people yelling at us for going 40 on a hill backed off when they got a load of Isidor. At first this hat had made me nervous too, but then I realized that Isidor was going to be visiting Los Angeles *as* J. J. Gittes. It was the perfect headgear for the trip.

There's nothing to see in Hollywood, if there ever was. The best thing about the real Hollywood is the bookstores, which are still replete and numerous. In one of them I found an amazing thing, a copy of the *Complete Report on the Construction of the Los Angeles Aqueduct*, from 1916, with a photograph of William Mulholland (the 'model' for Hollis Mulwray) opposite the title page. The real thing, right where it all really started. It cost thirty dollars, more than an entire day's budget for the Chandler Jaunt.

That was the most *Chinatown* thing that happened to us. We mooched around and saw some actor in a steak house on Hollywood Boulevard, if you can believe that. I showed Izzy the Beverly Hills Public Library, where I once saw a beautiful girl. In an unattainable, horrible kind of way. Bogart should have gone there – she would have flirted with *him*. One morning we drove out to Echo Park to look for *848 1/2 East Kensington*, where Ida gets killed, and of course it doesn't exactly exist, though I think we found the building itself. This is amusing to recall because I am no longer a person who could find his way somewhere, anywhere, in a car. How in hell did we get there? I asked Isidor if he wanted to go to Disneyland. *No.* But it's the happiest place on earth, I said, it says so right on the sign. *In that case, definitely no.*

We went down to San Diego to see what there was to dig up on Raymond Chandler, without whom, of course, there would be no *Chinatown*. He had lived in La Jolla, sort of set apart from San Diego, which is a handsome, sunny place stuffed with chain restaurants and sailors. We found his house, which looked as though it had been slightly modernized, painted gray, black and white, but with the same tall windows looking out at the Pacific we'd seen in a photo. Chandler wasn't happy there, and despite the sprucing-up the house looked as if it had been through something. You felt you were looking, rather rudely, at someone who'd lost his wife or been in a war.

In La Jolla there's a restaurant with a sea view, The Marine Room. Chandler used it in his work, calling it The Glass Room. He drank martinis there, so that's what we did. The next day we had quite Marlovian hangovers and made the disastrous mistake of going to the beach, a guy from New York and a guy who works in a *bookshop.* That night our skin was so red and painful that we couldn't go back to The Marine Room, or anywhere else. As luck would have it the Democratic National Convention was on TV from New York, and it was just an awful evening of dermatological agony, beer and the most endless speech by *Mo Udall.* It drove us crazy – Isidor was shouting things at the screen in Gittes mode: *Who is this bimbo? You're gonna MISS your train.* Etc.

The next morning proved to be the last of our intellectual journey to the heart of *Chinatown*. We went to a place for hamburgers that overlooked the zoo. When we finished, we paid and went downstairs and were suddenly *apprehended* and told we couldn't leave. A big surfer blocked the door. What is this? we asked. You guys think you can get out of here without paying? said the surfer. *Let me tell you something, pal*, Isidor began . . . Then this other surfer arrived from upstairs and said, What are you doing? That ain't them. Then they both left, without a word. *You forgot your check*, I said menacingly. There in the lobby they had those comment cards. Under HOW WAS YOUR VISIT TODAY? Isidor wrote: *I was falsely accused.*

In the car he turned into Escobar: *You wanna do your partner a BIG favor? Take him home. TAKE HIM HOME! JUST GET HIM THE HELL OUT OF HERE!*

Because of the expensive aqueduct report I'd bought and the all the Chandler martinis and a pipe I'd picked up at a cigar store in La Jolla, hoping Chandler had shopped there, I had no more money so we drove all the way to San Francisco that afternoon. Isidor was broke too and the next day he took the bus back to New York to learn some more Latin. My dad gave him $20 and a navel orange. 'What did you guys think you were doing?' he asked. As little as possible.

– Watching *The 39 Steps* –

– Is there anything else I can get you?
– A map of Scotland.
– Why Scotland?
– There is a man in Scotland I must visit next
if anything is to be done.

W here I lived there was no romance – only loud music and people in cars. So on the basis of this black and white Hitchcock movie, and a few lessons in folk music, I flew three thousand miles. My heart swelled at the sight of the Forth Bridge.

On Inverness station the rain came down in columns, many of the glass panes having been removed to some secret end. Or by acts of the deity or adversary. I left the last few oatcakes on the bar.

Is this the train for Kyle? I asked of a man who stood as though trying to dissociate himself from every aspect of the train. I therefore knew he was in charge of it.

I do not advise you to take this train. Danger abounds on the line. Such as, Sir, a great dampness that may sweep down from the hills. Also poor hygiene and catering facilities. Often there is a lack of oatcakes. His eyes became melancholic. *And there is the wait at Alt-Na-Shellach.*

He was no longer aware of my presence, so filled with doom and rain was he. I boarded the train. I was pleased to find it was a train with compartments. Humanity travels in comfort when cut up and prevented from feeling the whole of its unhappy majority. But to my disgust, in my compartment, there was an Antipodean, who began immediately to pester me with theories, his personal, of: gravity, vegetarianism, hygiene.

For years I've tried to convince my countrymen that we should be eating Roo.

In only a short while I was frantic. I got up and went to the buffet car. He followed me.

You don't need to change your clothes when you're travelling as long as you can shower once in a while. I use throwaway trunks. He produced what looked like a fruitcake tin.

I have heard of disposable underwear, I said, but . . . The smell of the Antipodean was pronounced. People winced as we walked in and made for the bar. In the hope of stoppering his gob I offered to buy him a can of beer. Of course this only made him more loquacious. As he raved on and on I was struck with the foul irony of being trapped with the Antipodean in the train as it began to climb into lovely country. The day had brightened; Ben Wyvis glowed distantly in the summer sunshine. Heathers tossed in the fore-meadows in a breeze sent specially to torture me and all within earshot of this lunatic.

I believe, my friend, Man can do anything, anything at all. Oh they say this anti-gravity idea is mad but it must be possible. I include the ladies.

Yes, I thought, Man can do many things. He can brush his teeth and bathe.

I locked myself in the toilet. But the window there was frosted and my need of scenery compelled me back to the compartment. He had fallen asleep and so remained until some Americans woke him by talking in loud, nasal voices about golf. Which, to their surprise, he had invented.

The weather became dark and wet again. The gentle rocking of the carriage lulled me into a romantic reverie which was interrupted when I suddenly perceived the funerary face of the aforementioned guard very close to mine.

Bring out your dead!

What! I jumped up.

Ticket, Sir. Going to Kyle?

I think so.

Think so!

Before I could ask the need for ironclad commitment he was taking the others' tickets.

A brief stop. I stood on the platform, admired the white wooden building. Its clover-shaped ventilating holes and unvegetated trellis. We started up and passed through a forest of pine and birch, then skirting a loch which shone mercurially in intermittent moments of sun. We picked up speed on a level strath, the line flexing lazily this way and that in a preternaturally pleasant land of hills, trees, heather and burns, until a station appeared ahead.

Alt-Na-Shellach! Twenty minutes!

Here, beside the place where the line briefly breaks into two, stood a battered station hotel and PUBLIC BAR. The driver and guard rushed for this in a fury. Some passengers climbed out and began walking up and down the platform.

Above Alt-Na-Shellach stood a mountain, moody and irregular. A forest of dark pines rose up.

In the bar I accosted the guard behind a glassware Martello of his own construction. Does my ticket include stop-over privileges? I poked it at him.

I do not advise you to stop here, he said, looking at my ticket as if he had never seen such a thing in all his life.

But surely I can get a bed here, and there is a hotel up the hill. What about crofters? You got any crofters around here?

Up the hill? he said. At this all conversation ceased and forty-nine frightened eyes crawled my length and breadth. *Crofters?* he said. All the color had left his face, even the subtle grays by which we had come to know him. But he regained his composure and punctured my ticket. *Suit yersel.*

The guide-book described Alt-Na-Shellach as 'a bleakly scattered hamlet'. It seemed what had been scattered in 1935 had by now utterly disintegrated. I made my way up the hill, where a sign told me there was a lodge. The station hotel would have done but I often seek a bed on high ground. There had been a tired small-clothes odour about the place which reminded me not faintly of the Antipodean.

I approached the portico of this Highland manor. The porch was of roughly-finished tree trunks, bristling with antlers. The day-man was astonished to see me and it took several minutes to convince him I wanted a room.

But where is your motor? he repeated.

Train, I came by train. He did not accept that I had walked from the halt. From the window I saw the train pull away.

How long will you be staying?

A day or two.

You mean you don't know how long you will be staying? He seemed outraged by the vagueness of my plans, an odd reaction from a man in the hotel trade. He regarded my violin case with suspicion.

Are you going to play that?

Someday.

I spent the afternoon looking out at trees from the window of my room. The Highlands changed themselves minute by minute, the land adjusting to a kind of fitful love affair with the sun and the great clouds. In the evening a little bell rang. There was Spey malt in the optic and fresh trout on my plate. I went to my bed very happy, wondering if the Antipodean had arrived at Kyle without being killed.

Deep in the night I conceived that something had grown on my neck. This was true. As it was preventing me from sleeping I attempted to lance it with my razor. Great torrents of gore rushed out which would not be stanched by tissue or all four towels. Holding my neck I stumbled downstairs whereupon the night-man, interrupted in paper-reading, jumped up on his chair and screamed at the sight of me. The antlered heads of all the brave dead of the foyer watched my life-blood ebb with great smugness.

The night-man wanted to telephone a surgeon at Ullapool, but I convinced him this would not be necessary as long as he gave me his entire box of plasters. They dated from an early era. The box was decorated with representations of short-haired nurses. Several hours later I fell asleep in my room which looked as if the embalmers had just finished up a pharaoh.

Breakfast was another handsome affair and while eating my ninetieth oatcake I decided, after a cavalier perusal of a map, to walk to a loch some ten miles away. The day-man assured me I could avail myself of the post-bus when I collapsed on the road. He regarded my neck with suspicion, obviously expecting it to open like a gruesome hydrant at any time. While talking to him I remained in the shadows under the staircase.

Full of oats and Arbroath fishes I set out. When I came to a rise I looked back and to my astonishment the whole parade of my private underwear was being hung on a line behind the hotel, my room having been ransacked to the purpose. Confused by such service I took time only to note that the hotel stood in a small grove, not the great forest I had imagined. Trees being feared by the landlords only slightly less than people.

Under a half black sky I walked, delighting at the way the hills would hint at their brothers and sisters, ever encouraging me with countless combinations of heather and rock, sunlight and cloud each minute.

After several hours the road became steeper. The freshening breath of the wind told me I was approaching the loch. But it did not appear and I regretted I had not brought some oatcakes with me, even though I was pretty well sick of them when I rose from the breakfast table. There were also some of them in the bathroom.

As I rounded a bend I heard a strange whining noise, such as one hears on the telephone on windy nights. A ram had got his beautiful curving horns caught in a fence. I approached to see if anything could be done, Aesopian visions flitting across my mind. I gave a tug at a strand of the fence, which had the effect of choking him. This drove him into a rage and he let out a surprising noise which gave me to understand that if I freed him, he would kill me. I backed down the road, thinking I would tell someone about him, so long as this exchange took place several miles away and I could impress my imaginary hearer that I must continue in the opposite direction.

I was thirsting and starving. After another desolate half hour during which rain set in, the freshening breeze told me I was approaching the loch. Still, it did not appear. But I was nearing a village.

A hotel presented itself. Abandoning my usual conceited reconnaissance of what-all a town has to offer, I fell against its door. Three men were seated at the bar, nooping over depleted glasses, engaged in some kind of secret local talk. I interrupted them. Hello.

Nod. Nod. Nod.

The entire row of optics were whiskies unknown to me. The barman put a quaich of oxtail and a plate of oatcakes in front of me; I asked for a half of malt and a half pint of Alloa.

The conversation turned on the subject of overtime work. Try as I might I could not understand the attitude toward it of the primary speaker. Whether he was complaining of it, wishing for it, or giving thanks for it. The nods and grunts of the other two were no help. I ventured to say, I have worked in a place where overtime was ingeniously carved away from me by introducing the costs of book-keeping it. You had to put in for thousands of hours of the stuff in order to come out ahead. This caused a wail to rise from my hearers and making honking noises they proffered complimentary glasses which appeared at my elbow.

Time was called. I made for the door in a hopelessly optimistic condition. One of the men called after me, offering a ride. No no, I aim to walk.

Suit yersel.

Outside the freshening air told me I was at last near the loch. However it did not appear and I decided it was time I faced my bed. It began to rain. As I passed the overtime hotel I had the urge to go back inside, but I knew this was not possible.

Soon I was cursing those men for their hospitality. The malt and Alloa were having damnable effects on my walking. I began to fear being run down, though there still hadn't been a single motor on the road. After an hour and a half I was miles from anywhere, moving with *tragicomic slowness*. A cabin appeared, an attendant portable sign placed by the side of the road: CRAFT CENTRE. TEAS. Tea, O *tea*, thank God for empire, it's a system. Knocks you down in Alloa, picks you up in Ceylon. Boldly I entered this dwelling.

What had been a sitting room, and perhaps still was, was filled with bolts of dirty tweed and tartan stuffs, dusty pots of heather honey and tea-towels terrible to describe. At the rear an elderly man slumbered against a hot stove. His eyebrows and the tails of his cardigan were just beginning to singe. Awake!

Slowly he came to. A beatific smile dawned on him

and putting his gnarled feet into a pair of Red Douglas baffies he came toward me at the counter. The heat was intense and inside me it reacted with the drams and the Alloa in a profoundly discouraging way.

Good afternoon. He swayed from side to side, his eyes watered. Pissed as I.

I'd like a cup of tea please.

Was just going to have a cup.

There followed the most hellish prolonged drama-turgy of tea-making ever. This man's aged condition and his enslavement to drink combined to introduce doubt and slowness at every turn. I couldn't bear to see the ungodly hysteresis with which his trembling hands sought the tea canister, with which he stared into its depths for minutes, hours. Yet such was my state that I could not look elsewhere in this shop, the entire history of bad souvenirs rioting in a nightmare of sickly colors and *petit-bourgeois* slogans. I tightened my knuckles on the edge of the counter and tried to clear my mind by thinking of something I knew nothing about: trigo-nometry. But the universe began to frolic and the hori-zon to dance and sing, sizzling in my ears. From various clangs and exclamations I gathered little progress was being made toward tea. Suddenly the enveloping whorl of my sickness was pierced by clear precise tones. I opened my eyes to find two Englishwomen engaged in studying the wefts of tea-towels but treating the propri-etor and myself with disdainful vigour.

You see. I told you.

With that they retreated, brushing at themselves in a way which suggested they thought the place full of virus. The man continued to fool with his equipment and I had to sit down on the floor to avoid plummeting to it. Some minutes passed.

Your tea, Sir. Och now where's he gone? Why the fucking bastard.

I managed to reach my hand up to the counter, which frightened him momentarily.

Ah there you are Sir. That will be fifty pence. And here are oatcakes which I hope you'll enjoy with me.

Which was worse, the sight of oatcakes or the discovery that out of comradeship or habit and I didn't really care he had augmented the tea with a tremendous helping of malt? I wondered if I should ever arrive back in my own life, or at least at its hotel. Some time later, I left. He had put his head back on the range to roast.

Outside the freshening breeze told me the loch was near. The tiniest black clouds carried quickly across the sky like the remnant puffs of a locomotive, each one drenching me demurely as it passed overhead. There was no sign of the vaunted post-bus and it was with but a grim idea of life that I walked toward Alt-Na-Shellach.

The evening was gray and a choking mist seeped out of the very rocks, covering the road with a spiritous foreboding. I felt lost in a tremendous world I had never seen before nor asked to be in. In the absence of sunlight the granite domes of Ross-shire revealed a chilling sepulchral personality and the stands of trees which had delighted my eye assuredly now contained mad things, professors with missing fingers, police.

Finally I could see, through the black thick end of the gloaming, some trees trying to hide my hotel. It began to rain in torrents and I had no heart to run – it was still a distance. As I turned up the drive to the hotel, the post-bus whizzed past me. A wave from the driver. Its merry horn. Next to an elderly lady in the back seat was the ram, staring daggers at me.

I approached the building. Everything in all the world was wet. A girl dashed outside at the back and snatched my wet underwear from the line.

The night-man was sitting at his desk. *A message for you, Sir.*

I opened the piece of paper. BRING YOUR VIO-LIN TO THE STATION TONIGHT. Where did this come from?

Out there, he said, indicating only the wider world. I did not believe him.

In my room my underwear was folded in a neat stack, discharging gallons of Victorian water onto my bed. A knock at the door. Yes?

You'll have had your dinner?

I took the note from my pocket. Why not? The rain had stopped and the monsters had eaten the mist. The moon shone through the firs as I made my way down the hill, toward little hatchings of light at the station. I put my head into the bar.

Next door, said the barman. *At the actual station.*

I nodded without understanding and went along to the stationmaster's office, which was illuminated. I found myself in a smoke-filled dastardly overheated room with twenty pinkened men and women, crustaceans on the boil. One was seated at a piano and there were violins on laps and in hands. Strong was the odour of Indian weed and oatcakes on a griddle on the coal stove. A little man came toward me.

Ah, you have come. Please have a chair and play with us. Songs of heather and hill.

You've muck all over you, said the stationmaster cryptically, *here and there. Have a dram?*

I accepted and the music began. We danced and marched all of Scotland, flew like desperate birds up and down the indigenous scale of the flatted seventh. We aroused plaidie-happed ancestors, declared war, drew tears with mournful ballads entombed in the earth like Iron Age men in bogs. Women sat and sang on every knee, bottles of malt filed into the Culloden of our guts. After joining in *The Braes of Balquhidder* in entirely the wrong key (E flat) I was emotionally enjoined to lay down my violin and more fully partake of the passive pleasures the evening afforded. This I did, my hands firmly held behind my back by one of the other musicians.

Deep in owl hour I was triumphally borne up the hill to my bed by three brave women of Scotland. One of them undressed me, one of them kissed me, and one of them divided my money between them.

– Ornaments on the Tree
of *White Christmas* –

I thought Bing Crosby was an actual vacuum tube, plugged in and glowing in the back of old radios and TVs. It was his voice. You'd look in there and he'd be humming. Smoking his pipe.

In middle age, I gained a new respect for *White Christmas*. Not respect – an entirely perverse love for it. Adrift and stateless, I somehow accommodated *White Christmas* as an antidote to this and as a talisman of my childhood Christmases. I don't think I was even aware of the movie as a kid. Our family didn't get a color television until just before those guys set off for the moon, and I'm not sure if *White Christmas* was being shown regularly on TV then. By the time the Revolution came along, things like *White Christmas* were looking pretty corny. They are. We had to have the Revolution, you know – otherwise we really would still be listening to Tennessee Ernie Ford and Perry Como. Doris Day might have made it to the White House. We were dying in Squaresville.

Boo Hoo

I have endured well over two decades of Christmas in the United Kingdom. Americans think Christmas in England must be like Dickens. It *stinks*. In 1985 I was marooned for *ten days* with only a cold for company during the joyful period when the English stop work altogether, as opposed to doing *practically* nothing, and suck sweeties while watching reruns of their abysmal television shows. In Scotland I was once arctically entombed in a house that contained for the festivities only a quarter bottle of Famous Grouse and a Black Bun. A Black Bun is like a *calzone* stuffed with raisins. If you eat it your head wobbles, you lose consciousness for a moment and your teeth zing so hard your dentist can hear it across the Atlantic.

Don't get me wrong. Christmas in America is no longer what it's cracked up to be; I could never go back. One winter in Arizona I stood eating my sandwiches looking out at the apartments of retirees. I was living through the off-season in a golf-oriented condominium. Do not ask why. It was The Holidays. I watched silver-haired grandparents attempting to stanch the flood of arguments, tears, mucus, vomit, ammunition and blood that is Christmas in America. These grandparents had thought everyone in the family would like to *come up to the mountains* and *have a fire in the fireplace* and *go for walks in the snow*. And their kids looked like they were going to divorce as soon as the courts re-opened and the grandkids were filled with horror at the emptiness and blankness of life at 8,000 feet. They had to be taken frequently to Walmart. That was their entertainment.

Red and Green

White Christmas is a treatise on the textures of the Fifties. The opening titles mean a great deal. Particularly the shade of the red background, in front of which are sprigs of green holly and the pleasing white of the 'Old English' lettering. (Americans are much better at Old English lettering than the English: that idea, again, that Christmas is essentially English and that it involves roasted poultry, hot chestnuts, cheeks ruddy from amateurish skating, charitable feelings and Old English fonts. Jesus Christ.)

This red is a brick red, and the green is dark and matte. These were the particular red and green of Christmas in the 1940s and 1950s in America. The red and green of cardboard Santas and their equally cardboard chimneys, the red and green of the displays in Macy's in *Miracle on 34th Street*, even though that's in black and white. You *know*. Garlands. Gift tags. Now Christmas is crimson and iridescent green or even blue, the reds tending toward magenta, greens that belong to bamboo or olives. Everything blinks and looks cold, like a cheap fairground. Instead of being given the colors of Christmas, we're injected through the eyeballs with the hypnotic, evilly fascinating colors of capitalism. It's a catastrophe.

White Christmas was made the year after I was born, so I couldn't have seen it or really comprehended it until 1960. Even though I know that the world looked like this right before I was born, I experience nostalgia for things I never knew, the world I must have absorbed in the womb. So it's not nostalgia at all but serious neurosis. This kind of nostalgia affects my generation of Americans totally and it's one of many things that make us politically useless.

The proper reds and greens continue throughout the picture, admirably balanced by Mrs. Kalmus's grays. Mrs. Kalmus wasn't on this picture. The Technicolor advisor was Loyal Griggs, and he was loyal to the Kalmus palette. There were grays in the dressing rooms and the hotel, with an odd orange look to the incandescent lights. The grays have to battle some surprising eruptions, like the turquoise dresses in 'Sisters', or the almost psychedelic luridness in 'Mandy'. In 'Mandy', there's a really perverted distortion of the red and green Christmas aesthetic. The colors clash luridly against a red background, ornate white armchairs or thrones the meaning of which is impossible to discover, and a surfeit of legs akimbo. As a kid, of course, you ignore the dance numbers.

They got poor old Edith Head to go along with this! She dressed Danny Kaye and Bing Crosby in as much gray as possible. In the dressing-room argument scene (in how many mainstream movies do you see the *male* leads in their underwear?) Danny and Bing wear carefully Technicolor-grayed t-shirts and underpants. They're not white and they're not dirty. One hopes. Nor are they disposable. They pack everything away in their identical trunks.

Repression HQ

Michael Curtiz opens a number of scenes in *White Christmas* with a louselike shot of women's legs – not in the first scene, of course, because that's with the US Army in Europe. But subsequently he likes to sweep along a pair of long limbs of the Fifties. What do they say, these dynamite gams? The war's over, come and get it? Women now on special, aisle twelve? Are these legs there for the DADS, who, after all, shucks, are paying for the family to get in the car, use gasoline and get to the god damn matinée, paying for 'em to see a movie called *White Christmas* during the *god* damn holidays. It's a war movie with showgirls, so show the girls.

White Christmas distils so much of the look of the Fifties and its repressions. It's full of paraphilias. Sex was out, really – it had to be buried under schmaltz – so you zap people with shots of fishnet stockings and *gather around the fire.* Genius.

There's a thread in the dialogue that goes on and on about eggs, and chicks, and mother hens, all having to do in some incomprehensible way with *reproduction*, which in the Fifties was the only meaning sexuality could have. (This might possibly have been better suited to an Easter movie, but what are the Easter movies? There's really only *Ben-Hur*, *The Easter Parade* and *Baby Huey's Great Easter Adventure*.)

A strange, clever erotica is at work in *White Christmas*. Have you ever felt a greater fascination with someone you were attracted to because it was a holiday? Because you had a few days off? Because the family beckons and the banks were shut? Think back.

Our lives are meaningless, so we want holiday love moments. Watch Bing help Rosemary down from her berth in the sleeping car. Look at their little eye-moment at the piano after rehearsal. Christmas can add uncertainty to love; then the moments when it is reaffirmed are even more Christmasy. Bing looks almost frightened when the curtain goes up on Rosemary in the Carousel Club – for one thing she's wearing a very sexy dress – she's ditched the red pj's. But later he's so relieved when she marches back on stage in the final scene at the inn after becoming convinced he's not a scheister. They wave at each other a little.

Rosemary Clooney is Betty. Vera-Ellen is Judy. Bing is Bob. Danny Kaye is Phil. Phil and Judy, Betty and Bob. These names fly at you from out of a magazine story. They couldn't be more perfect Fifties couples. They *insist*.

Bonhomie

American holidays clog you with bonhomie. At Thanksgiving the family is gathered together – look at your pretty cousin. Your pretty *second* cousin. Hallowe'en: woo woo! Valentine's Day? Valentine's Day has been in my lifetime turned from a modest schoolday exchange of little cards bought at the drug store to almost mandatory commercialized seduction – if your idea of seductive is a set meal of two indifferent pink steaks and a bottle of white zinfandel. The erotic potential of Easter is pretty minimal too unless you dig being made to wear dress shoes that are too small. The Fourth of July? Firecrackers and the simmering passion of a barbecue? Get outta here! But *Christmas* . . .

The eroticism at work in *White Christmas* is a triple whammy. It's a showbiz story, it's a romance *and* it's Christmas! POW! Showbiz lends an extra edge to romance; showbiz is a little bit naughty. A showbiz story allowed Hollywood to string the audience along with something sexy, but to satisfy the censors and the Legion of Decency this sexiness had to be defeated, or quashed by 'real' love, which is the case with *White Christmas.* Rosemary goes from cuddly (red dressing gown) to sexy (the green dress, the black dress) to (practically) married. The finale looks like a wedding. Between people wearing strange red suits.

White Christmas involves almost no snow, even though it's called *White* Christmas and there is an entire song entitled 'Snow'. A bit of snow falls in the last three minutes of the movie. I therefore conclude it is really about Christmas in California, about *me*. It becomes a rehearsal of everything *else* about Christmas: the brick red and the ivy green, the decorations (a kind of tissue paper bell you unfold), even the gift tags. The stabs at Christmas the desiccated make.

'Snow' is one of the best numbers. A wide and cozy club car on a nice American train heading for America's Winter Playground. Phil and Judy and Betty and Bob seem to have cleared the air of deceit for the moment; they sing about snow, but for whiteness there is only malted milk and napkins, or daiquiris being poured out by the bartender and a bowl of white popcorn. When did you last see popcorn in a movie, especially associated with romance? The love food of the Fifties. While singing 'Snow' they make a little winter scene for themselves by ripping up some pine decorations from the décor on the table (*railroad property*), strewing them on Danny's white napkin and holding Rosemary's blue scarf behind it. I lived through most of the Fifties and I never saw anyone do anything like that.

'Snow' is also a great number because it's such a *relief*: Bing, the Father Figure, has *relented* and they're going to Vermont!

Pleasure and fun have gone through such frightening, pressured changes since 1954 that it's impossible to imagine what's going on, or is supposed to be going on, between Betty and Bob in 'Snow.' It's the *beginning* of love, of attraction. That extra itch given to love by The Holidays. Judy: *'To see a great big man entirely made of snow . . . '*

There's no snow when the gang arrive in Pine Tree. Rosemary asks the stationmaster about it, saying she thought this was supposed to be New England's Winter Playground. The stationmaster should have told her Vermont is New England's *Celibacy* Playground.

Instead he just shrugs and says it was sixty-eight yesterday. (Not sixty-nine.)

Legs aside, the sexlessness in *White Christmas,* and what is supposed to be romantic, is startling. This is difficult to watch. No one, not Bing Crosby, Rosemary Clooney, Vera-Ellen, Danny Kaye, Dean Jagger or Mary Wickes can make the slightest advance at each other. They're layered under so many heavy Fifties duds and so much Technicolor that it's like watching different species thinking about *trying* to mate with each other and then not doing it. The skirts are as armoured as hoop skirts; Vera-Ellen in the window seat seduction scene looks like she's wearing a table for four.

When Mary Wickes spontaneously kisses Bing and Danny on the lips in gratitude for helping out the old General, it's like manna from heaven.

White Christmas is a menopausal concoction: the scenes alternate cold, hot, cold, hot, cold, hot. The sublimated emotions of the Fifties. Rosemary Clooney in her red flannel pajamas is *cozy*. But she's also a hottie. Then in the cast party scene, when she rejects Bing, she's in a luxurious green velvet dress. So it's the big freeze. In the last scene she's red hot.

White Lies

White Christmas is full of so many ideas about deception and confusion that by the time the idiotic misunderstanding that's come between Rosemary Clooney and Bing Crosby is resolved (she learns the truth about his selflessness by *watching television*, of all things) you really don't care. The whole thing abounds in lies, which seems Fiftiesish, but not very Christmasy. First the replacement general is sent on a wild goose chase so the soldiers can have a show. Vera-Ellen sends a letter to Bing pretending to be her own brother. Bing and Danny pretend to be Rosemary and Vera-Ellen so the girls can escape from the sheriff. The landlord is a crook. Bing and Rosemary pretend not to hate each other. Danny sneaks the girls the train tickets, depriving Bing of a bed, and tells them it was Bing's idea, then he lies to Bing about having lost the tickets. Rosemary lies about why she's looking for sandwiches. Bing and Danny try to hide their plans for an army reunion from the General. After eavesdropping, Mary Wickes emotionally distorts what she overhears and causes Rosemary to flip out. Vera-Ellen forces Danny into a pretend engagement. Danny fakes a serious leg injury. Even once Rosemary has decided Bing is OK, she hides her intentions from him. An entire former Army division is somehow hidden from the General until the last moment . . . This is Nixon level dishonesty.

Rosemary Clooney said later she never understood the 'confusion' between Betty and Bob: 'Why doesn't she just ask him?'

'White Christmas' the song existed before it was in *White Christmas*. It appeared in *Holiday Inn*, which in no way is a better picture, and became a gazillion-selling record – for years it was the best-selling record of all time. Carollers sang it on every block. Elvis did it. *Iggy Pop* did it. Last Christmas I got drunk and watched *Holiday Inn* and decided I'd always been wrong about it, that it's actually funny and has a plot that works. The next day I watched it again and I was *appalled* by it. It seems stuffed with crumby performances, especially the females and the guy who plays Fred Astaire's agent, and the Lincoln's Birthday number is in blackface! Nice.

Christmas in Connecticut, on the other hand, is a much better Christmas movie than all of them, though it too begins with a mawkish armed services back-story. It's got a great 'Hollywood Connecticut' house – to rival the architect's house in *Mr. Blandings Builds His Dream House* and the aunt's country home in *Bringing Up Baby*. Stone fireplaces, heavy beams, wide floorboards. A picture window. (This is all due, of course, to the fact that most screenwriters in Hollywood missed the east so much they could cry.)

The erotic chemistry between Barbara Stanwyck and Dennis Morgan is far better than any (if there is any) in *White Christmas*. She's leading one of those perfect New York existences where your lunch is brought to you from the restaurant next door by S.Z. Sakall. It's really Sakall's movie, as the proprietor of one of the most intensely loveable New York restaurants in the movies.

Ahhh, Restaurant Felix! It's at '325 46th Street' – ha ha. They liked to depict these cosy, relaxed New York restaurants, panelled in blond wood, as being below street level – which they often were (Manhattan rents haven't changed much). Booths, plate rails, ice water, butter, checkered tablecloths – what else? The restaurants in *Bringing Up Baby*, *The Thin Man*, *His Girl Friday* and *Ninotchka* could almost be the same one. Restaurant Felix is extra special because *massive roasting* is going on right there in the dining room. There's also Felix's excellent bow tie.

> – *Felix, bring us some wine, will you? Something very good but not too expensive.*
> – *Born in 1937, yes?*

A shot of the menu shows a caricature of Uncle Felix. There's marinated herring in sour cream and onions, gefilte fish, celery and olives. Chicken soup or chicken noodle broth. Hearts of lettuce salad – 30 cents. Lots of dishes *paprikás*. A half broiled spring chicken . . . $1.35. Wiener schnitzel $1.50. Blintzes, sandwiches, scrambled eggs. It's 1944.

There's also a bar, where Dudley and Sloan nurse little tiny martinis, waiting for Barbara Stanwyck. When she arrives she asks for a double martini, but she's whisked off to the table before the barman can give it to her. But then, before they bring the wine, Babs GETS the BIG martini.

Uncle Felix resolves everything in the end of *Christmas in Connecticut* by withholding braised kidneys from Sydney Greenstreet until he gives Barbara her job back. Keeping food from Sydney Greenstreet seems a pretty risky thing to do.

At the table in the dining room of the Columbia Inn, Pine Tree, Vermont, where Bing, Danny, Rosemary and Vera Ellen are having dinner shortly after arriving, next to the saltine crackers there is an elongated china bowl. In this bowl, sitting on ice, are butter, radishes, celery and black olives. I long for this bowl. It was on the table of every restaurant and hotel dining room I was ever in from 1953 till the Revolution.

Irving Berlin was pretty popular, considering he never did more than he absolutely had to. 'Sisters' is one of those numbers where you find yourself wondering what you will have for supper. 'The Best Things Happen While You're Dancing' is a real dose of the Fifties, really weird. Danny and Vera-Ellen, who are supposed to be attracted to each other, dance around a phallic lighthouse, and the lyrics go '*Things you would not do at home come naturally on the floor.*' Filth! 'Mandy' is almost indescribable: like *Holiday Inn* it ties itself in knots attempting to have nothing to do with *negro stuff*, as they would have said. All the Hollywood bullshit that preceded and inspired it is there.

Why Are These People Singing?

But can anyone really understand musicals anymore? What is the effect on your average twenty-five-year-old's brain when he or she encounters *White Christmas*, or any picture in which people suddenly depart reality and start singing something with a very tenuous connection to what they were just doing? It's hard to imagine that it makes any sense to them. Can anyone in the world today relate to *prancing*? If you'd pranced like the males in pastel neckerchiefs in *Seven Brides for Seven Brothers* on the real frontier, you'd have been eaten by the Donner Party. What does it mean to a modern person that Gene Kelly gets soaked in *Singin' in the Rain*? Come to that, what did it mean to Gene Kelly? To get *so* wet in the service of a bunch of pretty mediocre songs by Arthur Freed . . . but there you are again – Californians and rain.

Is the musical lost as a tool for understanding? Or even as a stratagem? It must be true that the variety of entertainment and art is shrinking. No one can grasp what's being got at in a musical comedy, can they? Aside from touring companies for hicks no one even goes to musicals any more, except in London and New York, where it's an ingrained habit, like Sunday dinner. It's an *order*. Similarly, dog races don't exist for most of us, and neither do waxworks, or playing with a hoop and a stick.

One may also wonder what younger people think when they see a *nightclub* in an old film – presuming that you can find a young person who will agree to watch an old movie. (A teenager of my acquaintance once stood up, after we'd started to watch *Harvey*, and announced, 'No! No more black-and-white movies with one-word titles!' He stuck to that.)

I knew about nightclubs because my parents went to them, or told me they had been. I doubt they were ever in one after I was born. There's a photograph of my dad, in uniform, in a nightclub in Bermuda, taken no doubt by one of the tired women in fishnets (enough with the fishnets already!) who used to show up at nightclub tables with a Graflex camera . . . I knew that a nightclub was a place where you sat at little tables and girls sold you cigarettes and you had drinks and a man or a lady came out and sang to you, and EMOTED while they sang, which is something that must strike people as fantastically strange today. It just seems so little – no flashing lights, no lysergic acid. Why would you even leave the house? What can the young possibly make of a big smoky room with a tiny orchestra of men in suits, and one person *singing a song*, to which the crowd is *listening*?

There is something strangled going on about Germans in *White Christmas*. Is Danny Kaye wearing a German field cap in the hospital? Traitor. Why does Bing suddenly start talking in a German accent when he comes at Rosemary with a tray of sandwiches? Does that make the sandwiches more attractive? The inn is, as Mary Wickes says, a 'Tyrolean haunted house'. Why is there a guy with a German accent amongst the US Army buddies attending the tenth reunion? Is he a spy? Is he an offering of postwar reconciliation?

The Romantic Glue of the Sandwich

The scene with Bing and the sandwiches, the prelude to the 'Count Your Blessings' number, is attractive for two reasons. First, the Fifties sandwiches, stuck with Fifties toothpicks and Fifties olives. The large stone pitcher of cool buttermilk and the beer taps at the bar. Inspired, Bing comes out with his unique sandwich theory: the kind of sandwich you eat at bedtime determines what kind of women you will dream about. It's not clear if Rosemary wants or expects to dream about women, but she's all smiles. She's supposed to be all smiles. In my stateless, anguished period I did like seeing this: it reminds me of many autumn and winter afternoons in many American houses, having a ham sandwich superfluous to my needs, and gazing out at a leaf-strewn yard.

Bing says to Rosemary *Let's gather around the fire.* I snap to attention. The Columbia Inn is very stylish in just that early Fifties way – there's a lot of fieldstone, a large open hearth designed to be sat around by the guests, surmounted by a sleek copper flue.

I have always been winter-deprived. When I was eleven we moved north. I was excited that we were now in a place that had seasons. My parents promised us that it would rain, even snow once in a while, and that in the fall there would be dead leaves. Perhaps best of all, our new house had a working fireplace. We did have fires occasionally in the first few years we were living there. Cosmetic fires. We burned Pres-to-Logs, made of compressed sawdust; you bought them at the grocery. I was always happy when these were part of the shopping. We struggled in our brave Californian family to have *fireside feeling.* In the earthquake of 1987 our chimney cracked, making it unusable, but by that time the weather was so hot that we'd stopped having a fire even at Christmas.

After not actually eating any sandwiches or butter-milk, Bing and Rosemary sing 'Count Your Blessings Instead of Sheep'. She's wearing her red pajamas, red dressing gown, and her white wool coat, something that it seems every woman owned in the Fifties. When they're finished, Bing gives her a little smile and then snatches his pipe out of his breast pocket and LUNGES for matches on a side table. To evade a kiss, he has to smoke immediately. He quickly envelops Rosemary in an atomic cloud of blue pipe smoke, in the middle of which she's still smiling and trying to say something nice to him. He certainly can't see her. She needs to be obscured because she is a hottie and he is attracted to her. They do kiss in the end, but this is very brief because the General wanders in and says a lot of nervous, embarrassed things.

Smoke If You've Got 'Em

The great thing about *White Christmas* is that everyone smokes. Bing, Danny, even a top General smoke smoke smoke. Maybe the title really refers to the immense cloud of cigarette smoke that surrounded everybody in the Fifties. Cartons of twenty packs of Camels were specially decorated for Christmas. But I'm exaggerating – Vera-Ellen doesn't smoke nor does the general's granddaughter. But Danny Kaye offers everybody cigarettes and puffs away like a street tough.

When I was a kid, every public building you went into smelled of cigarettes. I can remember the smell of the lobby of the telephone company in our town and the large urns filled with white sand and butts where you waited for the elevators. Once I saw the guy whose unenviable job it was to clean these out – he used a special little rake, leaving the sand and just some black streaks of ash behind.

Forties America must have smelled wholly of Lucky Strikes. But in the Fifties it was Sir Walter Raleigh pipe tobacco all the way. In *The Best Years of Our Lives*, there's an entire *wall* of Sir Walter Raleigh in the drug store where Dana Andrews loses his rag.

Danny Kaye smokes at the dinner table the first night at the Columbia Inn. Bing hasn't smoked yet so it's suspenseful for der Bingle pipeful fans! But the better movie for all your pipe-smoking needs is *Mr. Blandings Builds His Dream House*. Why, Melvyn Douglas is smoking a superb Dunhill (you can tell by the white dot) from the very beginning. In the scene in Cary Grant's living room, Melvyn gets free coffee and then takes tobacco from Cary's coffee-table humidor. When Cary imagines himself a country squire with a Great Dane, he's holding a shotgun and has a gleaming Great Dane-size pipe in his mouth. Melvyn has a pipe in his office but no humidor so you start to feel fishy about where he got that pipeful. Cary smokes his pipe during the depressing litany on the condition of his Connecticut house from Mr. Appolonio, the engineer, who smokes a cigar. Reginald Denny the architect has a pipe from the git-go, using it to point at various things on the plans for the new house, so that you wonder if he's getting little dots of saliva all over them. Melvyn arrives in Cary's office and hunts *rabidly* all over it for tobacco. Cary's not going to tell him where it is. Melvyn finds it, in a desk drawer. It's a big can, like the kind 'Surbrug' tobacco used to come in that you bought at the Wilke Pipe Shop on Madison and 48th. Melvyn also has a pipe going in the Blandings' living room when they argue about the mortgage and several pipes at the building site, then Cary smokes one at the office. They smoke pipes together when they get locked in the closet: *they use the same tobacco and they both desire the same woman.* Kinky. Mr. PeDelford the painting contractor has a cigar and his foreman Charlie a large Peterson 'system' pipe – he's the only pipe guy in the movie who's ornery, maybe because his pipe is too big for him.

On a wet night (the RCA Building in the rain) Cary is stuck at the office trying to think up a slogan for ham. He has to work hard and feel lousy so he smokes *cigarettes.* He, like Bing, actually uses the phrase *pipe and slippers,* saying to his secretary he'd always wanted to be home on the first rainy night of the year. Meanwhile Melvyn is at the house with Myrna, stealing tobacco! And he steals some more in the very last shot!

Meanwhile, Back in Vermont

The morning after Bing's kissed Rosemary and covered her with choking acrid smoke he has his pipe outdoors and lights the General's roll-up. But it's not the pleasant smoking, it's Bing's clothes. His hat has more than the usual jaunty crush. He's wearing yellow socks, a blue and red bandanna and a nice glen plaid jacket but he really does seem to have his pants on backwards. Some night of love – he's exploded.

White Christmas is the kind of movie you watch with a slight tremble – you're hoping that it will embrace you and entertain you in a genuine way so that you needn't be afraid of it or worry about it. Tricky: is the comedy funny enough? Is the warmth we feel for the General warm enough? In some scenes you think: these people really don't have any interest in each other, do they? You fret. And what is so great about war?

The finale is a full-blown rendition of the title song. The painted New England winter scene strung up by the soldiers in the middle of the war has now become real (sort of) as it's finally started to snow in the final few seconds. But *White Christmas* really ends for me when the Christmas tree center stage, blocking the crowd's view of the snowfall, is suddenly yanked by a rope and goes lurching unsteadily off stage left. *The wobbly tree.*

– Cary Grant's Suit –

North by Northwest isn't about what happens to Cary Grant, it's about what happens to his suit. The suit has the adventures, a gorgeous New York suit threading its way through America. The title sequence in which the stark lines of a Madison Avenue office building are 'woven' together could be the construction of Cary in his suit right there – he gets knitted into his suit before his adventure can begin. Indeed some of the popular 'suitings' of that time, 'windowpane' or 'glen plaid', reflected, even perfectly complemented office buildings. Cary's suit reflects New York, identifies him as a thrusting exec, but also protects him, what else is a suit for? *Reflects and Protects* . . . a slogan Roger Thornhill himself might have come up with.

The usage of calling a guy a 'suit' if you don't like him, consider him a flunky or a waste of space, applies to Cary at the beginning of the film: this *suit* comes barreling out of the elevator, yammering business trivialities at a mile a minute, with the energy of the entire building. The suit moves with its secretary into the hot evening sun where we can get a good look at it: it's a real beaut, a perfectly-tailored, beautifully-falling lightweight dusty blue – it might be a gown, you know.

I like thinking of it as 'dusty' because of what befalls it later. It's by far the best suit in the movie: the villains, James Mason and Martin Landau, wear funereal, sinister (though expensive) black, while their greasy henchmen run around in off-the-peg crap. 'The Professor', head of Intelligence, bumbles about in pipe-smoked tweed.

In 1959 we were a white shirt and black suit nation: the revolution was ten years off. There's a nice photograph of Ernest Lehman, who wrote this picture, sitting in Hitchcock's office, a black and white office of 1957, natty in a white shirt and black trousers. Some could carry off this look, but if you were *forced* to dress this way, say if you worked for IBM, it contributed only to the general gloominess of the age. You wonder if life itself was conducted in color then – even the 'summer of love' was largely photographed in black and white. Don't let anyone kid you: the Sixties were dreary.

Outside on Madison there, the white shirts blind you, but none of them is quite so white as Cary's. (As someone with experience in theatrical make-up, I have no idea how they kept it off these white, white collars. It drives me nuts.) Non-streaky Cary's daring and dashing in the most amazing suit in New York. His silk tie is exactly one shade darker than the suit, his socks exactly one shade lighter. In the cab he tells his secretary to remind him to 'think thin', which allows us to regard his suit, how it lies on his physique.

A friend of mine in politics said to me once, 'I love

wearing suits. They're like pajamas. You can go around all day doing business in your pajamas.' It has to be said that his suits were pretty nice, particularly so for *Boston*; whether he meant that he did his business half-asleep only his constituents could say.

The suit strides with confidence into the Plaza Hotel. Nothing bad happens to it until one of the henchmen grasps Cary by the shoulder. We're already in love with this suit and it feels like a real violation. They bundle him into a limousine and shoot out to Long Island, not much manhandling yet. In fact Martin Landau is impressed: 'He's a well-tailored one, isn't he?' He loves this suit. But next Cary tries to escape, there's a real struggle, they force all that bourbon down his throat . . . (He later thinks they'll find liquor stains on the sofa, but if there was that much violence why aren't there any on the suit?) Cut to Cary being stuffed into the Mercedes-Benz – he's managed to get completely pissed without even 'mussing', as they say in America, his hair. On his crazy drink-drive, the collar of his jacket is turned the wrong way round. That's *all*. He gets arrested, jerked around by the cops, and appears before the judge next morning and the suit and the shirt both look great. But this is the point in the movie where you start to worry about Cary's personal hygiene. Start to ITCH.

It's back to the bad guy's house, then back to the Plaza, looking good. I always hope he'll grab a quick shower in George Kaplan's hotel room – he keeps gravitating toward the bathroom. There's a good suit moment when he tries on one belonging to Kaplan, the guy he's looking for, who doesn't exist. Since these suits have been planted by the US Government, they're stodgy, old-fashioned, unbelievably heavy for a summer in New York, with *cuffs on the trousers*. 'I don't think that one does anything for you,' says Cary's mom, and boy is she right. She also contributes the joke that Kaplan maybe 'has his suits mended by invisible weavers', which *is* what happens to Cary's suit throughout the picture! His suit is like a mouse victim of repeated *cartoon violence* – in the next shot it's always fine.

Off to the United Nations, where the Secretariat looks even more like Cary than his own office building. He also sublimely matches a number of modern wall coverings and stone walls throughout the picture. He pulls a knife *out* of the guy the villain threw it at, but doesn't get any blood on himself. There's a curious lack of blood in *North by Northwest*; it must be all to save the suit, though they must have had ten of them, no? He evades the bad guys again and he scoots over to Grand Central Station, where they have, or had, showers, but he's probably too busy . . .

Cary's wearing dark glasses here, probably not too suspicious given it's summer. This is what's ingenious about this picture, at least as far as the SUIT goes – he's able to travel all over the country in just this one beautiful suit because the weather, the adventure itself, have been planned for the suit by Ernest Lehman! *It's the perfect weather for an adventure in this suit*, and that's why it happens.

At the same time, there's an effective CREEPI-NESS about the whole escapade generated by your own fear that in some situation Cary will be inappropriately dressed (Cary GRANT?) and this will hinder him, or that the thin cover the suit provides him will be pierced and here he's thousands of miles from home with not so much as a topcoat. The fears one always has of being too cold in a suit (Glen Cove, Long Island, even on a summer night) or too hot (the prairie, to come). Exposed, *vulnerable*. He does have some money though, we know that, so he could buy something to wear if he had to, assuming his wallet hadn't been destroyed if the suit had. But it would actually be too traumatic to see this suit getting totaled, way beyond Hitchcock's level of sadism. This feeling of exposure, having suddenly to make a desperate journey in just what you have on, comes up earlier in *The Thirty-Nine Steps* (book and movie) where Richard Hannay is alone in a desolate landscape in inappropriate town clothes, an evil-looking 'autogiro' spotting him from the air . . .

The suit holds for Cary a number of tools. It's so well cut you can't tell if he's even carrying a wallet (turns out he is). He goes all the way from New York to Chicago to the face of Mount Rushmore with: a monogrammed book of matches, his wallet and some nickels, a wrist watch, two cufflinks, a pencil stub, a hankie, a newspaper clipping, and his sunglasses (but these are shortly to be demolished when Eva Marie Saint squashes him into the upper berth in her compartment). All this stuff fits invisibly into the pockets of the most wonderful suit in the world.

Now he's sitting in the dining car with Eva Marie. He looks even better groomed than ever. With his deeply tanned, artistically manicured hands, he lights her cigarette. She's wearing a suit too, sober, fitting her 'profession', though with rather a low neckline.

Does the suit get crushed in the upper berth, even though his Ray Bans are smashed? No. Cary keeps his jacket on in the make-out scene that follows. The suit defines him, he's not going to take off that jacket. You know this feeling.

When Cary and Eva Marie walk from the train into the station in the morning, her dark suit, which was more like James Mason's the day before, now matches Cary in a strange way: as he's wearing a purloined red-cap's outfit, open at the neck and showing a triangle of snowy white undershirt, she has the same white triangle peeping from under her jacket. Two little innocent white triangles who spent the night together on the train. There might be an opportunity here in Chicago for a shower, you itch, but it looks like he chooses merely to loosen his shirt and have a quick shave, with Eva Marie's comically small razor. The suit was temporarily stuffed into her luggage while he made his exit from the train disguised as a red-cap. Has the suit suffered? Has it hell, it looks like a million bucks, his shirt still glows. But now comes the suit's greatest trial, the crop-dusting scene at 'Prairie Stop'. This begins with a nice suit moment when he and the farmer eye up each other's attire across the hot highway. Cary gets covered in dust from giant trucks going by (a deliberate and somewhat comic *attack on the suit*), sweats like a pig (or should, *we* do), has to throw himself into the dirt, gets sprayed with DDT, then practically gets run over by a tanker, grappling with its greasy undercarriage and writhing around on the asphalt.

After all this and having fled the scene in a stolen pick-up truck, Cary has only his hankie with which to make himself presentable at the Chicago hotel where he thinks 'Kaplan' is staying. Still, he's done a pretty good job – rather than all that stuff that happened to him it looks more like he's been teaching school all afternoon – just a bit chalky. His tie is still pressed and the shirt is white, even the collar and cuffs. You cannot violate the white shirt of America. You can kill me but you will never kill this shirt. By the way, Eva Marie enters this scene in a really luxurious dress – a side of her decadent double life with James Mason – and it's all pretty uncomfortable because now Cary is

a DIRTY MAN loose in civilization, too easily spotted
. . . But the *suit* gets rescued here! Eva Marie tells Cary
she'll have dinner with him if he'll let the valet clean
it! Cary tells her than when he was a kid he wouldn't
let his mother undress him. Eva Marie says, 'You're
big boy now.' In one sense Cary's growing up, from an
essentially childish, meaningless New York executive
and, you suppose, a playboy, into a man taking charge
of sorting his life out. He *grows into his suit* over the
course of the adventure. In another sense, though, he
maybe has a BONER – he's been sniffing round Eva
Marie and suggesting a skirmish. This is all very good,
totally neurotic movie dialogue – I don't know who
suffered more, the writer, the actors or the audience
in those days.

So Cary takes off the suit, goes into the shower,
she gives it to the valet, and she splits! The suit is not
there, so Cary is not there. We get to see that he wears
yellow boxers, another sign that he's a daring guy in a
'creative' profession – whew! (In the shower he *whis-
tles*. Long time ago, huh?)

Once Cary gets to the auction gallery, the suit is
perfectly restored – that valet is some little 'sponger and
presser'. He gets in a fist fight (no blood), is arrested,
taken to the airport, put on a plane to Rapid City . . .
The next day it's hot as blazes at Mount Rushmore, but
the shirt is clean, the suit's fantastically smooth, a hot
breeze rustles it a little. The monument itself is wearing a rock-like suit in deference to Cary. He's turning

into a rock, too (ignore what I said up there). Eva Marie arrives in mourning, essentially – black and gray; James Mason is in some kind of weird English country gent get-up, to suggest I guess he's never been one of us, he's not long for these shores now. She 'shoots' Cary: no blood, of course, as it's a charade, but wouldn't you think the CIA would use *fake blood?* How else are they going to put this over on James Mason? He's not an idiot. But you can't do this to the suit or Cary Grant or the audience.

Now the suit is in the woods for the 'reconciliation' scene with Eva Marie. This suit doesn't look too bad in the woods, and you reflect that Mount Rushmore seems a formal national park, there were a lot of people dressed up in the cafeteria, paying their respects . . . it's 1959, remember. Cary gets punched out for trying to interfere between the Professor and Eva Marie, AND WHEN HE WAKES UP THE SUIT HAS BEEN CONFISCATED! The Professor has locked him in a hospital room with only a TOWEL to wear (though you feel a lot of relief that he's had his second shower of the picture). He's not going anywhere! This then is the real act of cruelty: the Professor brings CARY GRANT a set of *hideous* clothes from some awful 'menswear shop' in Rapid City, you can just imagine the smell of it, Ban-Lon shirts and cheap belts: he gives him an *off-white* white shirt, a pair of black trousers, white socks and icky black slip-ons.

You get the creeps and realize this whole thing is about insecurity, exposure, *clothing anxiety.* When Cary escapes out to the window ledge he's inching his way along in a pair of *brand new slip-ons which may not fit!* Your feet and hands start to sweat at this moment and they don't stop. But make no mistake: *Cary is now in black and white*: everything is CLEAR to him, and he acts decisively OUTSIDE the suit, in order to be able to win it back. For us there's the confusion and disgrace of a badly-dressed Cary: the situation is now a real emergency.

Now he crawls up the stone wall of James Mason's millionaire's hideaway, which looks so like the face of the office building in the beginning, the rectangles of a snazzy suit. And in this white shirt with no jacket, Cary is a sitting duck in the bright moonlight! *A New Yorker without a jacket on.* It is too frightening.

Delightful to discover that in the end, when Cary and Eva Marie are on the train back to New York (she in virginal white nightie), he's got his suit back. He's not wearing the jacket (woo-hoo!) but he has a nice clean white shirt and those are definitely the suit's trousers and his original shoes and the gorgeous socks. *Now* he knows how to wear that suit.

I managed to acquire a pair of trousers several years ago that were somewhat like Cary's. They weren't tailor-made, and weren't the same quality of material of course, but the color was really close and the hang of them wasn't bad. And they turned out to be Lucky Trousers, very very Lucky. Until I burned a hole in them. The veneer of civilization is thin, boys. Exceeding thin.

My Prizes: An Accounting
Thomas Bernhard

Written in 1980, *My Prizes: An Accounting* is a caustic account
of Bernhard's experience of receiving nine major awards. What
for most writers is a moderately nerve-wracking experience,
followed by the euphoria (and relief) at having won, Bernhard's
hated of everything to do with literary prizes is laid bare in this
mordant, yet viciously funny, memoir by one of Europe's most
famous literary *enfants terribles*.

On Dogs: An Anthology
Introduced by Tracey Ullman

Introduced by Tracey Ullman (an inveterate adopter of strays),
this beautifully illustrated anthology traces the canine's
extraordinary journey from working animal to pampered pet.
Includes contributions from Shakespeare, Alice Walker, James
Thurber, Miranda Hart, Will Self, J. M. Barrie, Jack London,
A. A. Gill, Brigitte Bardot, John Steinbeck, David Sedaris, J. R.
Ackerley, Virginia Woolf and more.

Mourning Diary
Roland Barthes

Roland Gérard Barthes (1915–1980) was a guru among
literary theorists. Raised by his mother, Henriette was the
most important person in his life, and yet Barthes's devotion
to her was unknown to even the closest of his friends. Written
as a series of notes on index cards, as was his habit, *Mourning
Diary* shows us how Barthes began reflecting on a new solitude
only days after his mother's death by recording the impact of
bereavement as he struggled to live without her. The result
is 330 cards that are at once intensely personal and entirely
universal.

Wandering Jew: The Search for Joseph Roth
Dennis Marks

Joseph Roth, whose many novels included *The Radetsky March*, was one of the most seductive, disturbing and enigmatic writers of the twentieth century. Born in the Habsburg Empire in what is now Ukraine, and dying in Paris in 1939, he was a perpetual displaced person, a traveller, a prophet, a compulsive liar and a man who covered his tracks. In this revealing 'psycho-geography', Dennis Marks makes a journey through the eastern borderlands of Europe to uncover the truth about Roth's lost world.

Frida Kahlo and My Left Leg
Emily Rapp Black

At first sight of Frida Kahlo's painting *The Two Fridas* (1939), Emily Rapp Black felt a connection with the artist. Like Kahlo, who sustained lifelong injuries after a bus crash which led to the loss of her right leg, Rapp Black is an amputee who learned to hide her disability from the world. In *Frida Kahlo and My Left Leg*, Rapp Black examines how she began to recognise – and make sense of – aspects of her own life, and experience, via Kahlo's extraordinary art. Drawing on the art, letters and diaries of Frida Kahlo, Rapp Black takes the reader on an exhilarating journey to understand the place of disfigured bodies in our air-brushed world.

Thoughts of Sorts
Georges Perec
Translated by David Bellos, Introduced by Margaret Drabble

Celebrated as the man who wrote an entire novel without using the letter 'e', and another in the form of a vast jigsaw puzzle, Georges Perec found humour – and pathos – in the human need for arrangement and classification. The essays in *Thoughts of Sorts* explore the ruses by which we find a place in the world. Is thinking a kind of sorting? Is sorting a kind of thought?

Humiliation
Wayne Koestenbaum

With a disarming blend of personal reflection and cultural commentary, American artist and cultural critic Wayne Koestenbaum walks us – at times cajoles us – through a spectrum of mortifications, in history, current events, literature, art, music, film, and in his own life.

Happy Half-Hours: Selected Writings of A. A. Milne
Introduced by Frank Cottrell-Boyce

A delightful selection of writing from non-fiction books and articles by the ever-popular A. A. Milne, many of which haven't been in print for decades. Introduced by the prize-winning children's author Frank Cottrell Boyce, this volume is an ideal gift book, bringing A. A. Milne's brilliant non-fiction back to the spotlight.

On Cats: An Anthology
Introduced by Margaret Atwood

Introduced by Margaret Atwood, who was a 'cat-deprived young child', the writers in these pages reflect on the curious feline qualities that inspire devotion in their owners, even when it seems one-sided. Includes contributions from Doris Lessing, Edward Gorey, Mary Gaitskill, Ernest Hemingway, Caitlin Moran, Nikola Tesla, Muriel Spark, John Keats, Lynne Truss, Guy du Maupassant, Rebecca West, Hilaire Belloc and more.

The Wrong Turning: Encounters with Ghosts
Introduced and Edited by Stephen Johnson

Why do people love ghost stories, even when they don't believe (or say they don't believe) in ghosts? With contributions from M. R. James, Alexander Pushkin, Charlotte Perkins Gilman, Tove Jansson and more, this uniquely curated anthology brings together some of the most chilling stories from around the world.

How Shostakovich Changed my Mind
Stephen Johnson

Winner of the 2021 Rubery Book Award

In this powerfully honest and brilliant book, BBC music broadcaster Stephen Johnson explores the impact of Shostakovich's music during Stalin's reign of terror and writes – at the same time – of the extraordinary healing effect of music on the mind. As someone who has lived with bipolar disorder for most of his life, Johnson looks at neurological, psychotherapeutic and philosophical findings, and reflects on his own experience of how Shostakovich's music helped him survive the trials and assaults of mental illness.

Alchemy: Writers on Truth, Lies and Fiction
Introduced by Iain Sinclair

Reality versus fiction is at the heart of the current literary debate. We live in a world of docu-drama, the 'real life' story. Works of art, novels, films, are frequently bolstered by reference to the autobiography of the creator, or to underlying 'fact'. Where does that leave the imagination? And who gets to define the parameters of 'reality' and 'fiction' anyway? In this riveting collection, introduced by one of Britain's most celebrated writers, Joanna Kavenna, Gabriel Josipovici, Benjamin Markovits, Partou Zia and Anakana Schofield debate.

Questions of Travel: William Morris in Iceland
Lavinia Greenlaw

The great Victorian William Morris was fascinated by Iceland, which inspired him to write one of the masterpieces of travel literature. In this fascinating book, which is part memoir, part prose poem, part criticism and part travelogue, celebrated poet Lavinia Greenlaw follows in his footsteps, combining excerpts from his Icelandic writings with her own eye-witness response to the country.

The Mystery of Being Human: God, Freedom and the NHS
Raymond Tallis.

For forty years, Raymond Tallis was a consultant NHS. In this brilliant collection, Tallis brings his signature intelligence and razor wit to the questions that define us as human: Do we have free will? Can humanity flourish without religion? Will science explain everything? And can the NHS – an institution that relies on compassion over profit – survive?

*All titles are available in the UK, and some titles are available in the rest of the world. For more information please visit www.nottinghilleditions.com.

A selection of our titles is distributed in the US and Canada by New York Review Books. For more information on available titles please visit www.nyrb.com